CREATED IN HIS
IMAGE

ISBN 978-1-950252-07-7

CREATED IN HIS IMAGE

BY SUMMER MCCLELLAN

OTHER BOOKS BY SUMMER MCCLELLAN

The Impossible Marriage

What Can I do for God?

Satan Has No Power Over You, You Belong to Jesus Now

Faith What is It?
Jesus is Our Example

Passing the Tests of Life

Light and Darkness

Grace What is It?

Broken Hearts

To *Rhonda*

When I consider Your heavens, the work of Your fingers,

The moon and the stars, which You have ordained,

What is man that you are mindful of him, and the son of man that you visit him?

For You have made him a little lower than God,

And You have crowned him with glory and honor,

You have made him to have dominion over the works of Your hands;

You have put all things under his feet,

All sheep and oxen---

Even the beasts of the field,

The birds of the air,

And the fish of the sea

That pass through the paths of the seas.

Psalms 8:3-8

TABLE OF CONTENTS

INTRODUCTION

I came to know the Lord when I was fourteen years old. First, I met Jesus. He walked through the bedroom door and spoke to me. He told me He loved me. His presence felt like pure majesty. His voice was so compelling to me, I felt it contained everything.

Although He is the King of all Kings and the Lord of all Lords, He came to me and told me He loved me. He did not have to tell me twice. I wanted His love with all my being! This encounter immediately changed my life forever.

My parents certainly were relieved; they did not know what to do with me, I gave them so much trouble! They had tried everything, especially my dad. He had grounded me, one time I was grounded to a chair for a month. He had also spanked, yelled, and gave me a belt whipping which I deserved. Nothing seemed to work.

I was so thrilled to have actually met Jesus! But a couple of days later, the Father spoke to me. I heard Him too. His voice was deep and rumbly. His voice spoke to the very center of my being. He told me to consider myself part of His family.

You cannot imagine what these two encounters meant to me. You see I considered myself worthless. I felt like trash, and I treated myself accordingly. I had believed the voices in my head that I was worthless, and nothing mattered, until I heard God's voice. He valued me.

Soon I heard the Holy Spirits voice too. He spoke to me through things, like words to songs and little tugs on my heart.

He was leading me and teaching me.

I had the most marvelous secret inside of me! I knew God! I knew the actual God of the universe and He loved me!

Soon after I got saved, I was in the car with my mother when a car turned in front of us and a collision was unavoidable. I could see that we were doomed. But suddenly it was like a giant hand came and pushed our car out of the way. I was shaking with terror at the narrow escape but amazed! Amazed because I knew that a miracle had just happened. God had actually, miraculously saved our lives.

My secret felt so amazing. I felt a little bit cocky. I knew God. He loved me. And He was not going to let anything hurt me! I had God all figured out. He was good, and He loved me. He was real, and I could just pray, and He would probably do what I wanted Him to do because He was so nice. I kind of felt like I had God in my pocket.

I decided to read the whole Bible and I did. I read it constantly. Now I knew everything written in the Bible and I had God all figured out and most people did not even know Him! It felt good, very good.

Except, what I did not realize was God had made Himself very small to reach me. I really did not know much about God at all. In fact, I now realize that I knew next to nothing. Now over forty years later, forty years of seeking to know Him better, I only know I was nuts to think I was some kind of expert on God. He let me go on like that for a while. Now I know that He is so much bigger and stranger and better and more powerful and beyond what my mind can contain.

I think I must have matured a little bit because after more than forty years of seeking Him I feel I barely know Him. I long to know Him better. I now know enough about Him that although I long, earnestly long, to see Him, that thought also terrifies me.   He is so much more than I ever thought He was, but there is something else too.......I am created in His image, so are you.

There is so much about God I need.....NEED... to learn, but there is so much more to me, I need to learn also. I am not as simple as I once thought I was either.

I am no longer smug, and I do not think I have God in my pocket. Now I would describe it more like desperate. I desperately want to know God better. I complain to Him all the time. You used to talk to me more! But I realized that when He wants to tell me something He does. What is difficult to hear is all the stuff I want Him to tell me.

I keep finding out God is different than I first thought, He is bigger, and He keeps getting bigger and bigger and bigger. Not that He is changing but I am realizing the magnitude of our God.

This book, Created in His Image, is a subject that is so awe inspiring and so exciting to me because the more I find about God, the more I find out about myself. I was created by Him and in His image.

Volume 1

LET'S TALK ABOUT GOD

Chapter One

THE TRUTH OR A LIE

I love the documentary called The Atheist Delusion. It can be watched on YouTube. Even if you are not an atheist it opens your eyes. I feel a surge of faith watching that movie. I realize that even though I have never been an atheist, the pall of unbelief that hangs over the earth affects me and the truth presented in the film renews the wonder of God to me.

Even as a believer the movie causes a new faith to arise in me. In the film, Ray Comfort, the maker of the film interviews several people. The first question he asks them is if they are atheists and they all say that are and they tell him they don't believe in God. The film clips to each person in his interview and their answers. They all believe in evolution. Several of them are college students and are being taught this in their classes.

When I hear people say they don't believe in God, it

upsets me. Hearing all these people spout off that we are the product of a big random explosion and then somehow chemicals just started evolving and forming cells and the earth and stars and planets and plants and animals, well.. it irks me. I wanted this guy to show them good.

But the movie was not like that at all because the heart of this man making the movie was not to make them look bad, but to open their eyes. And that is what he did. I wondered how he would deal with this; would he pull out a bunch of scientific evidence that would blow their minds? He didn't. He just pointed out some simple logic.

"Can a book write itself? Can the letters on the page just form themselves and the pages come together, and the binding appear and the words all just make sense randomly?"

Each one said, "No, of course not."

Ray agreed, it was impossible, because there was a plan a design, so there was a designer behind it. Then Ray simply points out the design in them, their DNA is a book, a plan and a design for each individual. It is a design that is so intricate and complex in detail that if it was in book form the information would be enough to go around the sun and back. And that is just one human. Every human, animal, flower, tree, every living thing has DNA so intricate and so complex in design that it is mind boggling.

The plan in each cell is a complete plan of every system and organ of the body, from the magnificent structure of the eyeball, the heart, the lungs, to the color and texture of the hair and every part and function of the body. It is a plan, a blueprint, much like a computer program but infinitely more complex! And it is in every living thing!!!! Ray pointed out that this would be many times more difficult than a book writing itself. Everyone agreed.

Ray continues his conversation with each person with simple logic on the subjects of hell and sin and God's answer to these. By the end of the documentary none of those he is interviewing are still atheists. I felt I was witnessing a miracle. I was seeing these proclaimed atheists trading a lie for the truth. Light was coming on in their eyes and a change was taking place. It was absolutely thrilling to me.

By the end of the interview one of the young men said he wanted to pray and did so at once right on camera. Several others said they would pray when they got home, and one said he wanted to go to church.

I watched amazed. They went from unbelief to faith before my very eyes. And there was a change in me too. I went from being irritated with these people to feeling such love and hope for them. In fact, for several days after watching I kept them in prayer, asking God to continue the work in them. It was so exciting to me, like watching a birth.

I was amazed about several other things also while watching this movie and I want to tell you about them. One was Ray also interviewed a top leading atheist and showed clips from another. They amazed me because they were so afraid of the truth. They were not like the people Ray talked with, open to listening to the truth.

The famous atheist that Ray interviewed was asked if a book could write itself and instead of answering the question, he immediately started blabbering about the Bible being written by peasants who didn't know much about science. Then he started saying design is an illusion. His argument was about a snowflake. A snowflake was not designed, it looks designed but is produced by the Laws of Physics.

I wanted to scream because he was pitiful. Laws of Physics! The words came out of his own mouth. The universe is governed by laws, design, not chaotic chance. It is pure insanity what this man teaches! He seemed afraid of Ray.

The other top atheist they showed clips from was having a debate with a priest and what he was saying was so ludicrous that the audience started laughing at him. The confusion he was in and was trying to perpetuate was so evident. He couldn't understand why the audience was laughing and looked confused.

I felt amazed again. These are the men whose ideas are being taught in schools and others are holding them up as examples??!! They were tripping over their own arguments; they were so ludicrous. I felt that they were not unbelievers at all but just had a seething anger against God for some reason.

But here is the big summation of this whole thing to me. To believe in evolution, the lie, makes everything meaningless. There is no design order or meaning. There is no right and no wrong, no anything, just chance. There is also no accountability, and nothing matters. Just sing and do your own thing, which is a lot of people's philosophy.

But to believe that God designed each of us and everything about us so intricately would take us to another level. If God so designed just the plan for our body with so much detail and with such a deliberate plan not leaving out the most minute detail, would He not much more have designed a plan for our lives also down to the most minute detail?

Suddenly we go from nothing matters to everything matters, a lot! Each day, each hour, each second, they all matter. We have a purpose and a plan that God has designated for us. He is a God of incredible detail; everything is planned

16

and designed within a perfect plan. We have been designed and made intricately for a divine purpose and we have a divine role to play in this huge cosmos we live in, and we cannot live as if there is no design.

And if we were to miss that purpose which we are so intricately designed for, that would be the greatest loss that we could possibly imagine. It would be to miss our destiny and our purpose.

God has created everything around us, but His crowning creation is us. We are created in His image, in His likeness. There is nothing else like us in creation.

There is a responsibility to believing in God. The responsibility is to our designer and finding out just what He designed us to do and to follow His plan. If we were all to follow His plan, earth would become heaven. And someday it will be.

Our Father Who is in heaven, hallowed be Your name. Your kingdom come your will be done on earth as it is in heaven. Matthew 6:9-10

ChapterTwo
GOD IS BIG

When I got saved it felt like I had God all to myself. He belonged to me. He was with me all the time and in every conflict, at least at first, He seemed to be on my side. A few times my treatment of others aroused His anger and when He told me to apologize and when I said, "no" He told me again in a voice that could shake the earth. {Advice from Summer don't ever say no to God]. But even then, I felt God was mine full time, He was always near.

I was having a little trouble with God though. He wasn't always answering my prayers like I was asking Him too. I had to become a little more persuasive, that was one of my specialties, conniving and manipulating to get my own way. It actually seemed to me that God was just bent on doing everything the hard way. I stepped up the whining and complaining. I thought God was supposed to be making everything in my life perfect. Somehow God seemed to have lost control of things because things were not perfect.

I had an epiphany one day. I actually realized that God was smarter than me and He actually must have some kind of reason for making my life so hard. I just could not imagine what it could be or why. I decided to take it by faith and just believe there was some good reason. I started to realize God did not think like I did at all. His ways were really hard to understand. But as I matured a little, I actually realized His ways were higher than mine and I needed to trust Him.

More epiphanies came, I started to realize something, there are more than 4 billion people on this planet, a huge number. God can actually hear each and every one of them praying to Him at the same time. He knows each and every one intimately and He just makes each one of us feel like we are His only kid.

This thought made my head swim. How could anyone keep track of four billion people, even God? I realized He was so much more complicated, bigger, intelligent, unexplainable, than I could possibly imagine. I mean I knew He was big and powerful, but this was mind boggling. I started feeling a little less smug and like I owned God. In fact, I started to feel like I really had no concept of God at all.

And then there is this thing called outer space. The universe is so vast that distance is measured by things called light years. That is how far light travels in a year. I am going to write out that number for you a light year is about 5,878,499,810,000 miles. The distance of the universe is thought to be about 93 billion light years big. In miles you would have to multiply that number I wrote by 93 billion.

This universe God created is huge. That makes God huge. God is everywhere at once, there is nowhere He isn't.

That is a lot of space that God is occupying!!!

The Bible says He calls the stars by name. Would you like to know how many stars there are? Scientists believe the number looks something like this, 1,000,000,000,000,000,000,000,000. That is a lot of names, but not just names, places, large places.

There is no way for us to comprehend just how big God is. We have no way to fathom it. All we can say is He is much bigger than we think He is. God is everywhere all at the same time. He is at every place in the universe; the universe exists in Him. He is the life in everything, even His enemies and nothing has life without Him.

A small church I used to attend years ago would have testimony time and people could come up to the microphone and say something. One night a man came up and said a good friend of his that had died appeared to him in a dream. He asked His friend who was now living in heaven, "What is God really like?"

His friend just replied several times, "He is big! He is big!"

God is big and much more complex than we realize. His presence can be terrifying. He is powerful but we have yet to realize just how powerful. He is holy but we have yet to realize just how holy and He is big much bigger than we can fathom.

The day will come when we will stand before Him. It will come. We have to come to grips with that fact and live accordingly. He is going to weigh our thoughts, our words, our motives and our deeds. The big thing to remember is not to do what you think is right in your own eyes. That will not work.

In order to please God, we must do what Jesus did, our

example. He only did what God showed Him to do. He did God's will for Him. He told us He only did what He saw the Father do and His words were God's words. Jesus got up early to pray every day and He found out God's will.

God is very big but His plan for the universe includes you. It is your responsibility to come to God, on a daily basis, and follow His plan for your life and not your own.

In order to do this, we have to believe that this huge God who governs this immense universe and even calls every star by name, knows what is best for you. That He created you for a purpose and a plan within His great and huge plan. Then we need to live accordingly.

Chapter Three

THE TRINITY

For there are three who bear witness in heaven: The Father, the Word, and the Holy Spirit; and these three are One. 1 John 5:7

God is made up of three distinct personalities, they are three, but they operate as one. They are God the Father, Jesus and the Holy Spirit. Jesus is still sometimes called the Word in heaven because that is who He was before He became our Savior.

They are all three very important to us. We need all three. They are all three present with us and all three speak to us in distinct voices. They all three love us they all three help us and they all three are our God. We are to be baptized into all three.

Go therefore and make disciples of all nations, baptizing them in the name of the Father and of the Son and of the Holy Spirit, Matthew 28:19

Let's talk about each of them and look at each one.

The Father

The Father is all knowing, and all powerful. In Him everything exists. He is present everywhere and that includes the past, the present and the future. When I say He is all knowing that means ALL. He sees from the farthest distances in space down to the tiniest particles of an atom.

He sees inside of us, and He knows every thought and every motive. There can be absolutely no deception with Him. His presence can show up every thought and motive.

I have experienced His presence in this way, and it was absolutely terrifying. He is so pure and so holy that my words, my thoughts and my actions were utterly repulsive next to Him. I literally quaked and shook in His presence. As terrifying as this is, it is also so marvelous! Our Father is absolutely good and holy, pure and righteous. I really wouldn't want God to be any other way, although it means I have to change.

I am a great deceiver and manipulator. I always was. I was always whiny and sick and wrapping my parents around my finger with headaches and stomach aches. I even fooled myself into believing my own excuses to myself. This did not work with God. I tried it, of course but He saw right through me. We stand completely laid bare before the Father. I actually tried to manipulate the Father, but it didn't work.

Our Father is Love. He is true love, not like the flimsy

excuse of love that we have. Everything He does is out of love; all His actions are redemptive. Even His judgements come out of love and redemption because it is impossible for Him to respond any other way. We just found out the Father knows us completely, but He still loves us.

We have no idea the depths of the love of the Father, but again, that does not mean we can manipulate Him through His love for us. We have the responsibility on ourselves to do our part in our own salvation. Millions die and go to hell. They put their selves there, even though God loves them.

When I was pulling my manipulation stuff with God, I dug in my heels and refused to budge. I was going to play my games with Him like I had all my life. My self-pity, manipulation and self-destruction tricks had worked with my family …..but it wasn't working with God. He wouldn't budge. He let me know I could dig in my heels all the way to hell. He told me many had before me.

Uh-oh!

I did not want that! I realized I had better change. God expects maturity from us. I had to stop playing my games and grow up.

God Is Light

Our Father is light. Light is amazing stuff. It is energy but it is also more, eternal things are made of light. God is light. There is no darkness in Him, and He allows no darkness in heaven, not so much as a shadow.

The Father sits on a massive throne in heaven. He exudes blinding light and massive power. Those who have witnessed this sight and have written or told about it all describe the same thing, a huge throne that is surrounded by a rainbow. The light is so bright they cannot see into it. The waves of power and glory coming from the Father are so overwhelming they can barely lift their heads.

Huge angels are flying about the throne crying out holy. Some angels resemble blow torches and burn with huge flames and a pure sound. The place is noisy, with lightnings and thunders and loud noise, the whole place shakes.

Out of the Father, a river flows. It begins from His throne and flows throughout heaven. It is called the River of Life. Beautiful gems that come from the heart of the Father can be found all throughout the River of Life. They flow from the river which winds throughout heaven. It is a River of healing for those who arrive from this fallen world and need to be restored.

Our Father is also just. He is not a dictator who rules on a whim whatever He feels like that day. God is completely just. He follows His own laws and never violates them. People say God can do anything, but that is not true. God will not ever violate His nature or His word. He follows His laws, and His word is always true. Once He says something it becomes so.

Our Father is the head of the Trinity. Jesus taught us to pray to the Father in His name, and when we get to heaven it is Jesus who will present us to the Father.

The Word, Jesus

When I was first married, I had a Jehovah's Witness come to my door. I heard a knock at the door and as I was walking to answer it, the Lord spoke to me and said, "Do not let her in." I answered the door and there was a lovely young girl about my own age. I only opened the door a crack and was intent on getting rid of her. Instead, she drew me into a conversation about God. I told her I did not believe what she was saying but she drew me in and got me into a conversation.

The wind was blowing, and it was cold and as she stood there shivering a voice in my head said to me, "You are some Christian, letting that young girl stand out there in the cold."

I fell for the deception and opened the door and let her in. Suddenly an older woman appeared also and followed her in. The two of them and I were in a conversation about Jesus' deity. I told them Jesus was God. They told me He wasn't and turned to John 3:16 and read the verse. *"For God so loved the world that He gave His only begotten Son that whosoever believeth on Him would not perish but have everlasting life."*

"See," she said, "Jesus was created. It says He was a begotten Son."

The conversation went on for a few more minutes, but I got so angry, at their words against Christ deity, I was about to heave them out of my house. Sensing my hostility, they left. A few hours later a stream of demons entered my home. I tried to pray them away, but they wouldn't leave. I had let them in. They began to attack me with unbelief about the deity of Jesus. It was a horrible thing to go through. I finally got rid of the demons by going to a nearby revival and getting prayer.

There is a reason why Jesus is called a begotten Son and that is because Jesus had to become one of us to save us. He changed forms, from the Word to the Son of man. The apostle John understood this.

In the beginning was the Word, and the Word was with God and the Word was God. He was in the beginning with God.

26

All things were made by Him, and without Him nothing was made that was made. John1:1-3 and verse 14 says, *And the Word became flesh and dwelt among us, and we beheld His glory, the glory as of the only begotten of the Father, full of grace and truth.*

Jesus had to change forms to become our Savior. He had to become a human and be born into this fallen world. It was the only legal way to retake the earth and us. He became the second Adam. He became the Son of God.

This is absolutely amazing. Jesus has changed roles to become our High Priest, our Kinsman Redeemer, and our Savior. This is an eternal position. The love and humility Jesus showed is unfathomable. Jesus has restored us to the Father. We lost that in the Garden of Eden, but Jesus regained that for us. Jesus is the only way to the Father, there is no other way.

Jesus is Wisdom

Jesus is also Wisdom. He is the One to go to with the tough problems. He has unbelievable wisdom. Spending time with Him will increase our wisdom and knowledge. But remember the wisdom of God is foolishness to the world. He is not a get rich quick scheme or the ticket to an easy road as some seem to think.

Our Intercessor

Jesus is also our intercessor. He intercedes on our behalf to the Father. I learned this firsthand. I wrote about it in my book, *Satan has no Power Over You, You Belong to Jesus*

Now. I had been suffering from demonic oppression for years and I had kind of just learned to live with it. But it kept getting worse. I prayed, I rebuked, I prayed in tongues, I would go forward for prayer in church and get prayed for, but everything seemed to make it worse.

My nights were filled with terrifying visions and nightmares.

One night I had enough. I awoke to a terrible sting and there was a demonic spirit on my pillow that looked like a scorpion. That was just too much. I knew it wasn't supposed to be like this. These demons were supposed to go in the name of Jesus. I decided I was going to go to heaven in prayer and tell God on these demons that weren't submitting in Jesus' name, I could not take it anymore.

So, I closed my eyes to pray, and I started saying I am going to heaven, I am marching up to God's throne. I tried to picture it but all I could see was grey smoke. I was determined so I just kept marching through the grey smoke on my way to God's throne declaring I was going to get to His throne, nothing was going to stop me.

All of a sudden as I was marching through the smoke, I bumped into someone. I looked to see who it was.

It was Jesus!

I was very happy to see Him. I wanted some help; I wanted Him to comfort me. Well, I began to tell Him what was going on but before I could even finish, He turned, and He ran to the Throne. He threw himself down before the Father, He began fervently praying for me in what almost seemed like agony. I stood there amazed, just absolutely amazed. I would have settled for a hug, but He took on my struggle.

I immediately fell into a beautiful peaceful sleep which I

had not had for a long time. My nights had been pure torment. I was surprised when the next night the trouble returned, but the answer was soon in coming. The Lord led me to a man who was experienced in spiritual warfare that helped me. Soon the problems were dealt with, and the torment ended.

Jesus prays for us. He intercedes before the Father on our behalf. He also did this for Peter. Remember that Jesus told Peter that Satan had asked to have him to sift him as wheat. Jesus then told Peter, but I have prayed for you. Satan wants to sift all of us like wheat; he also petitions the Father and demands Him to allow him access to our lives based on his legal rights. We really need Jesus praying for us. We have an Intercessor before the Throne!

The Holy Spirit

To me the Holy Spirit is the most mysterious part of the Trinity. He is nameless and faceless. His voice is so quiet it is almost indistinguishable. Sometimes when He speaks to me it is just a knowing and not so much a voice. To me the Holy Spirit has a lot to do with speaking in tongues. The day the Holy Spirit came on Pentecost was the day they began speaking in tongues.

I had never heard about speaking in tongues in my life. I had never even heard the gospel until we stopped going to our old stuffy Congregational church that taught us you went to heaven if you sat through their boring stuff every Sunday.

After we moved out of town my parents started visiting churches to find a closer church. They got tired of driving so far to church every Sunday. They found one they liked that was close, but it was very different than the Congregational church. They taught baptism by immersion. It was radical compared to the church we had gone to. The only thing was it was all they taught. They had an altar call every Sunday for water baptism. They did not even pray a salvation prayer; they had you confess Christ and get baptized.

I actually did not get saved in church. I got saved at home in my sister's bedroom, but I did get baptized the next Sunday at the church. But our church did not believe in anything else. In fact, anything else was forbidden.

We found out about the Holy Spirit from a book, a Frances Hunter book. A Catholic girl from school loaned me a book by Frances Hunter. My mom and sister and I all read it and we got hooked on Francis Hunter books and started buying our own, although our Pastor saw the book while visiting and warned us not to read it. We kept buying her books and eventually got to the one called, *Two Sides to a Coin*.

It was about speaking in tongues. I was transfixed. I had never heard about speaking in tongues and the baptism in the Holy Spirit, but I wanted it! I started praying for it. I didn't speak in tongues that day, but I did feel like I was floating on a cloud. I wanted to speak in tongues! I wanted it, I wanted it, I wanted it! So did my twin sister Carol.

After we had prayed and longed for the Holy Spirit for several months my dad took a job in another city about three hours away. That was the year I started tenth grade in school. Carol and I found out there was a church in town that believed in speaking in tongues.

We begged our parents to take us there and they did, although they were reluctant. Carol and I went forward and got prayer at the church for the baptism in the Holy Spirit and a week later on the same night we both started speaking in tongues. It was bedtime and I was in my room, and I got it first. I ran to tell Carol and she immediately started praying in tongues also.

We were so happy. Every day after school we would race to our bedroom and spend hours in prayer, praying in tongues. We cherished the gift of the Holy Spirit and speaking in tongues. That was forty-one years ago. I feel like we are just scratching the surface of the gift of the Holy Spirit.

Let's talk about the Holy Spirit. The Holy Spirit is God Himself. The Bible tells us the in 1 Corinthians 2:10-11, *But God has revealed them to us through His Spirit. For the Spirit searches all things, yes, the deep things of God. For what man knows the things of a man except the spirit of the man which is in him? Even so no one knows the things of God except the Spirit of God.*

The Holy Spirit knows what is inside of God. Think of the magnitude of God. He knows everything in this vast universe, because it is all made by Him and exists in Him. The Holy Spirit is like a giant search engine on a computer, He knows absolutely everything there is to know about everything in the entire universe. He also knows everything that is inside each of us.

I have experienced this while I am writing books. He remembers things I have long forgotten. As I am writing He reaches out and pulls up a memory and it goes in the book. Sometimes I balk because it is too personal and then everything stops, I can't write another word until I put in what He wants to say. I don't know if I could write at all without Him.

God has put His Spirit inside of us who believe. He comes to live within our spirit, the part of us that is born again.

This is a new thing. This is beyond comprehension. God is no longer with us but in us. This is a gift. A gift that contains all the power and all the wisdom of the universe living inside your spirit.

Well why are some Christians so ungodly then?

Because our spirit is encased in our soul and our soul needs to be dealt with. Some people have a weak and tiny spirit, and they are ruled by their soul. The areas of our souls need to be broken and pruned and turned over to the Spirit. The Holy Spirit is still a great mystery to me. I know I want to know Him better.

{Also, the Holy Spirit is a little scary to me because I don't want to accidently blaspheme Him. One of the devil's biggest lies and he has pulled this one on me too, is that we have blasphemed the Holy Spirit and lost our salvation. The thing to remember is this, if you still care you then haven't done that, those who do that no longer care.}

I don't know if we will realize on this earth or appreciate the fact that God lives inside of us, the Father, Son and Holy Spirit. The Trinity all three are One and they are God, but they are three distinct persons, and you are created in Their image.

Chapter Four
THE THRONE

God's official place is the Throne. He is seated on the Throne in the Throne Room in heaven. But He is not glued to the Throne as some people think. The Throne Room is a meeting place.

The Throne Room is the most happening spot of the whole universe. This is the spot most to be desired to be, not only for us but also for angels too. It is a gathering place to come and worship God. But it is more than that it is the ultimate of the ultimate, where the universe is run.

There are many magnificent beings in the Throne Room. There are many kinds of angels, some which are huge with huge wing spans, others that burn like torches, there is a vast assortment of angels. Also, there are the hosts which are like an army, they are fearsome beings. Humans are there of course, most of those whose lives on earth are finished but some appear there from earth. Also, there are other types of beings, heavenly beings like the four living creatures and the twenty-four elders.

The Throne Room is described in scripture, and it has also been described by many witnesses who have visited heaven. Let's talk about what it looks like.

The Throne Room is a glorious place. It is elevated and can be seen from a great distance away. It is huge, hundreds of millions can gather there at once. The room is so large it is hard to determine its size, one witness thought it to be a hundred miles wide and fifty miles tall, others don't try to estimate a size they just say it is huge with millions and millions gathered there.

The Thrones

As they enter the room the glory coming from the Throne is overpowering. It hits like a gust of force of power and blinding light. The throne itself is elevated, on some sort of pedestal and there are two main seats, first the Father's and Jesus' seat is on the right. They have been described as plain and box shaped like a high back chair and dazzling white.

Anna Rountree speaking of the Throne, mentions in her book, **The throne on which the Father was sitting was bejeweled with intangibles: righteousness, justice, holiness, mercy and other virtues.**

Blinding Light

The Light coming from the Father is so bright He is not completely visible. Many see only His feet which are huge and

His hand. From His waist upward is blinding light. The dazzling light although white contains the spectrum of all the colors of the rainbow which appear in the light. The brilliant light bathes those present and also comes off in waves of glory, mighty waves rolling over those present, in love and joy and peace.

Clouds and Smoke

Also billowing clouds which are also sometimes also described as smoke are around the throne. Others have described seeing fire also. Flashes of lightning come from His presence, it is seen in His robes and throne and the sound of thunder. The lightning also comes from the clouds that are billowing from His presence.

The Rainbow

A beautiful rainbow also surrounds the Throne of every color. The colors have been described as beautiful and vivid. The colors begin with white, then gold, then reddish gold and reds, purples and blues and ending in green. The living colors also emit qualities and sounds, and smells and angels come in bathe in the glory of each color.

Power

There are massive amounts of energy in the room. The energy comes in and out of God with a mighty sound, "WHOOSH."

Richard Sigmund in his book, *My Time in Heaven* says,

The glory He was clothed with radiated from Him, sounding like millions upon millions of dynamos of surging current.

Whoosh. Whoosh. There was just surge upon surge of power.

Jesse Duplantis describes the power also, in his book, *Heaven Close Encounters of the God Kind.*

I heard a sound, *Whoooooosh!* There was a massive amount of energy in that place. That's the only way I can explain it. It was God's power! You hear that noise, then the energy goes back into Him. There is smoke and power and noise—the place is noisy!

There was a cloud that looked like smoke going up from the Throne and I heard that massive sound, *Whoosh*! It was power like I never experienced in my life.

Angels, Living Creatures and Elders

Above the throne huge angels circle around, they have a wingspan of maybe thirty feet, and they are calling out, "Holy, holy, holy!" They are huge and they add to the awe and wonder of the place. Also, around the throne, in the burning brightness are angels called Seraphim that burn like blow torches. A sound of total purity comes from them as they burn with holy brightness.

There are stairs that lead up to the Throne. In front of the stairs are the four Living Creatures. They are majestic beings. The four living creatures have eyes in the front and back and are looking all directions. Each of them have six wings. One looks like a lion, another looks like calf, the third

36

looks like a man and the fourth like an eagle in flight. These beings are also bright with blinding light, and they represent the four divisions of animate creation. These four living creatures hold golden bowls which they present before the throne. The bowls are filled with incense which represents the prayers of the saints.

There are twenty-four smaller thrones before the throne of God which belong to the twenty-four elders. They are ancient, wise and bear authority. They are also in the bright light. They have white hair and wear crowns on their heads.

The Lampstands and the Altar

In front of the Throne are the seven lampstands. They represent the Holy Spirit. I have heard them described as about five feet high with flames burning out of them, similar to the Seraphim, like blow torches.

Also, in front of the throne is an altar with hot coals. In chapter 6 of the book of Isaiah when Isaiah was in the Throne Room an angel touched his lips with a hot coal off this altar.

The Sea of Glass

In front of the Throne is the Crystal Sea or Sea of Glass. This is a huge area that serves like a ballroom floor. I have heard it described like a glass floor with water running underneath of it. It is blue and very beautiful. It is in a large oval shape.

Also, a river proceeds from the Throne, I am not sure where the water goes to, but a river flows out throughout heaven from the Throne, the River of Life of course.

The floor past the crystal sea is a marble floor with threads of gold running through it. We know this because when Jesse Duplantis was there, one of our witnesses, he spent a lot of time looking at it because he was so overcome by the presence of God, the power, the glory and the brightness he could barely life his head and he got a good look at the floor! He said it was beautiful.

It is Noisy!

I love the fact that the Throne Room is such a noisy place. I absolutely love it! Even though I am a shy person, I am a noisy worshipper so I will fit right in! In fact, I was visiting my daughter's church the pastor came after me and told me I was too noisy.

I hope you are not offended by noise in church because the Throne Room is noisy!

Jesse said, **"There is smoke and power and noise—the place is noisy! And angels are hollering."**

Isaiah said, **"The posts of the door were shaken by the voice of him who cried out, and the house was filled with smoke."**

The noise literally shakes the place!

Another witness describes hearing music, instruments with singing and the sound of thunder.

And don't' forget the whoosh, whoosh of all that power going in and out of God, and the sound of giant blow torches from the Seraphim and the seven lamp stands. Now add millions of saints singing and instruments and you have got a lot of noise! Good noise!

God Sounds like Thunder

When I used to live in Lakeland, Florida we had thunderstorms all the time. In fact, the area is the highest area in the nation for lightning strikes. The clouds there get so low that the storm is literally on top of you. When I lived there the thunder would wake me up in the night and the ground and the house would literally shake.

I loved it because in my half-asleep half-awake state of mind I would picture myself before the Throne of God and the sound effects and rumbling made it so real. I never opened my eyes, but I would worship God and hear the rumbling and it seemed I was in the Throne Room.

We should never be offended by the sounds of people's worship. When people abandon themselves in worship and let out a cry to God, the atmosphere in the room changes. It changes because the glory of God enters through the sound of their voice. They literally usher in the glory. That is one of the reasons I get loud in worship sometimes, I feel the glory and it is delightful.

The Throne Room also gets quiet too. In Revelation 8:1 John tells us there was silence for about a half an hour.

The Glory

The Throne Room is a glorious place. The glory is so strong not even everyone in heaven are prepared to go there. It is too overwhelming, and they have to wait until they are conditioned to the atmosphere. It may take a while. Those who worship often will be more able to go.

It is hard to describe in words the intensity of the Throne of God and the power surrounding it.

Lingering Glory

The glory from the Throne Room rests on the angels and people who go there. I can tell when an angel enters my house from there. I can feel it. It is different from the angels who are present all the time. The angels who come from the throne room are charged with energy and I can feel the voltage as they enter the room.

There are sometimes that I have felt that glory on me, also. I know I have accessed the Throne Room and that feeling lingers on me for days afterward. It is the most wonderful feeling. The best way to describe it is to describe the opposite.

Have you ever had a feeling of dread that you just could not shake? You don't know what is wrong, but it just hangs over you as you go through your day? Well it is completely the opposite. It is a strong feeling of well-being that just keeps overtaking you.

I had an experience like that one time when I took my daughter Joy down to Morningstar School of Ministry to go to school. She was only seventeen, but she was determined to go, and she was going by faith, and that is what it took, faith. She did not have much money and neither did I. It was an eighteen-hour drive down there and I did not want her to take it alone. So, I decided to drive down with her and take a bus back.

We had some trouble getting down a tire went flat,

.and we had to pay for a tow and a new tire with the little money we had. When we got there Joy had to find a job right away to pay for her expenses. I had just enough money to get her a blow-up mattress to sleep on and I bought her some bologna and peanut butter and jelly and bread to eat until she got a job.

I was really having a hard time, leaving my seventeen-year-old daughter far away with no money and I had no money to help her, and I spent all I had getting her there.

She was subletting with three other girls who were also going to school. When I found out they all had cell phones and there would not be a phone in the house for Joy to call home and Joy did not have money for a phone or could not even get one because she was under eighteen, that just about pushed me over the edge. I just wanted to bring her home and forget the whole thing!

Joy was determined to stay.

Before my bus ride home, I had time to go to a meeting at Morningstar with Joy. It was a meeting with Lou Engle and a bunch of kids going around the nation protesting abortion. Now I have been a Pentecostal for my whole adult life, and I have seen some wild worship, but this was really wild. It was nuts and I loved every minute of it. It was hours of wild worship, and it was different, but I did not care I joined right in. I just kept thinking if my Pastor saw this bunch, he would think we were all crazy! I am not even going to try to describe it, but I felt like we were right before the Throne of God.

The next day I had to leave my daughter there, in a big city, alone. I got on the bus and had a horrible ride back. It was the week of hurricane Katrina, and the buses were being sent down to that area so there was a shortage of buses.

It was horrible we were overcrowded on the buses, and I had about four inches of a seat. Then on the waits in between in the bus stations I could not sit and relax because there were not enough buses. I had to wait in a line for hours because I had to try to get on the next bus out. I couldn't be late because I had to get back for work.

I was scheduled for a fourteen-hour day at work the day after I got back, and I could not miss it because I was broke! It took about thirty hours to get home and I had gotten no rest. My ankles were swollen, and I was way past tired. I just wanted to get home and go to bed.

After a grueling 30 hours I got to town and my husband picked me up. When we got home and went in the door, he mentioned that Joy's school had called. They needed a notarized permission slip faxed that night or Joy would miss the camping trip which was the first week of school.

I couldn't believe he hadn't told me while we were in town. {my husband does not do details well, that is my department} So I jumped in my car and rushed to town before the store that did faxes closed. I got down the road and my clutch went out.

I got out and ran back home {on foot, swollen feet}. Got my husband and pushed the car home with his car. Then I took off in his car and got the permission slip faxed. Then finally I got to go home and get to bed and the next day I had to work fourteen hours!

It was a hard time! But all through it I had the most incredible sense of well-being. It clung to me from that worship service. It lasted for days. As miserable as I should have been and I was physically miserable and conditions were hard, but I had this wonderful lightness and joy I could not shake. It did not have to do with circumstances. It was the glory was resting on me from being before the Throne. It lasted for days. I kept asking myself, "Why do I feel so good?"

The Throne Room is such a wonderful place that accessing it leaves us with an overwhelming sense of buoyant joy and peace.

The Events

The Throne Room is a place like no other. Its size is massive. The beings, huge angels flying and yelling praise add to the excitement. And the four living beings, strange but beautiful creatures, are shouting and holding bowls of incense. Other angelic beings are so pure they dwell in fire and burn like blow torches! And God the Father, Himself dwelling in light that is inexpressible covered by a rainbow which shimmers from His glory. Thunder and lightening's and rumblings, smoke and fire and power and millions in worship!

What a place! What a glorious place! This is where our God sits, this is His Throne. In all the universe this is the best place to be.

In the Book of Revelation, we see huge events happening in the throne room. The book of Revelation describes events in heaven that affect earth. There is the scroll being opened and with seven seals. There are seven trumpets and seven bowls of wrath, all these future events are going on before the Throne.

Sometimes visitors to heaven will describe other events. Jesse Duplantis tells about Jesus stepping out of the glory of the Father and preaching a sermon. Jesse was surprised what a fiery preacher Jesus was. Many wonderful things take place at the Throne.

Other Places

There are other important places in heaven also. The Bible describes a court, and a judgement seat. There are different courtrooms. Other people who have visited heaven describe other throne rooms, there is more than one. There are many official places that God occupies.

I also think God must have an office, maybe a big desk where He does business and maybe He sees people privately. There is a reason I think He may have an office. It has to do with something that happened when I was a little girl.

When my twin sister Carol and I were about three or four we decided to make God a picture. Well sort of a picture it was more like a thing. We glued and colored and created an artwork for Him. I remember we even got into the cupboard and got into the muffin papers.

This was a three-dimensional artwork. We were so excited as we worked. We were excited to make God a gift. When we were done, we left it on the dining room table for Him to come and get in the night. We went to bed giggling with excitement, we were so anxious for God to come and get His picture thing. The next morning, we raced out of bed and down the stairs and into the dining room expecting the thing we made to be gone. We were heartbroken to find it still on the table.

Many years later I thought of that, and I asked God about it. I told Him I know You don't operate that way, but you should have come and got our artwork.

Immediately God showed me a huge billboard. I mean huge! There must have been millions of pictures on it all made by children. He treasures the artwork that children make Him. God has a billboard! A billboard where He lovingly pins each picture made for Him.

No, our artwork did not disappear on earth, but it did appear on a huge bulletin board in heaven! All I saw was the billboard and not even all of that, but I have it pictured in his office, near His desk where He can look at it often.

Well, back to the Throne Room, the most special place, a place so glorious and powerful that not everyone in heaven can visit because of the extreme amount of glory and power. This is the official place where God is seated and where the universe is run.

John the disciple saw it and describes it in the book of Revelation. Many people have visited this holy place and written about it also. I look forward to the day when I will see it for myself, the Father, Jesus, the Thrones and angels, the smoke with lightening's and thundering's, the rainbow the burning torches the huge angels the power and glory, and the multitudes worshipping God! I would rather be there than anywhere.

Better is one day in Your courts than a thousand elsewhere; I would rather be a doorkeeper in the house of my God than dwell in the tents of the wicked. Psalm 84:10

Chapter Five
GOD IS A GIVER

God is so generous. It is His nature to give. It is His joy to give. He gives and gives and gives and gives. And He has a lot of people to give to, but His giving doesn't run out. God gives what is good. There are times He allows testing, and we wonder why He isn't giving but, it is for promotion. All good gifts come from God.

Don't let the amount of people on earth that God is giving to throw you off guard and cause you to feel like one of the crowd. It is not like that with God. It is like you are the only person on earth. I don't know how it does it but that is the way it is with God.

Everything you have is from God. Your life, your body, your family, the world you live in, the possession's that you have, even your pets it all comes from God.

Now some of you may be thinking different things. Some of you may be thinking, "I have worked hard all my life for what I have got, it is not from God!"

I will deal with you first. I read a book one time written by a very successful real estate agent. She was a top seller and very prosperous. She sold a lot of homes, and she was living in a beautiful home. Someone said to her that everything she had God gave her and she got angry. She was one that felt she had worked hard and made her own way and said so. She argued that she had worked hard for what she had, and it had not come from God.

She was wrong, and God heard her. From that day on for a whole year, until she came to God and surrendered to Him, she never sold another house. She worked and worked and never sold a thing. She came to realize everything she had come from God. This same lady sold everything she had, including her magnificent home and entered the full-time ministry. She gave everything back to God.

Then there are others that say, "I have been poor my whole life, I have nothing. What has God given me?"

I was in that position, poverty. I know about that one. For years we did not have enough. We frequently ran out of food, wore old clothes, drove an old car and could not afford repairs. I needed everything. At one point for about six months, we went on welfare, and I felt like we were kings we had been so used to living on less.

I never felt angry with God during that time because He rescued me continually. It was always a struggle, but He always came through for me. I would not have survived without His care, and I learned a lot about faith and miracles.

I also learned that just because I was in poverty did not mean it was God's will. Poverty can come for many reasons; it is like a curse that needs to be broken.

Divorce releases poverty over a family or stealing, or many other sins. Satan comes to steal kill and destroy and he has somehow gotten a legal foot hold in many lives that blocks God's provision, whether from an ancestor or from the person themselves.

Tithing and giving break poverty. Gratitude and faith also break poverty.

God is a giver, and He has given you plenty, and not just physical things. God puts gifts and talents inside of us. He has given each of us a part of Himself and His attributes. We have been given gifts and talents to use for fulfillment and purpose. These are gifts from God.

Some of us are artistic and some musical some of us are scientific and some analytical, we all have some special things deposited inside of us by God. God is so multi-faceted, and He put some of His qualities in each of us. When we look at others, we are looking at a little bit of God because He puts Himself in each one.

I also want to mention that we have an inheritance coming. This inheritance is eternal, and it is more glorious than you can imagine at this time. The very least in the Kingdom of Heaven has an inheritance more glorious than the richest person that ever lived on earth. But our greatest gift, is that God has put Himself in us. It is more than a gift; it is a divine mystery.

So, it is God's nature to give. He is a generous giver. He is a joyful giver. He is a need meeter. And we are created to be like Him. We are created to be givers. It is who we are. We were not created to be greedy or stingy or hoarders.

Let me ask you something, have you ever met a stingy person who was happy? Have you ever met a generous person who was not happy? It is in us to give.

There is an exchange that happens in giving, a multiplication. Giving love to God is a supernatural event. An exchange of energy and power takes place, sort of like an explosion, a good explosion, an explosion of good.

When the Father gave His Son and the Son laid down His life, love gave, and love gave. There was a release of energy, an exchange of power, an explosion of resurrection power. It was a breaking off of evil and a release of good, through giving. There is something about giving we have yet to learn, something about giving in love, joyful giving, God kind of giving.

The Father and the Son have displayed Their giving for us. It is an explosion of light and power that freed us. It is something we can step into and join. We can lay down our lives to Them in love and the exchange continues to multiply and grow. Giving, in love, releases power and blessing and increase.

We were created to be givers also. It is a part of who we were created to be. It is also a commandment to give the tithe, a tenth of what we earn.

Somehow when I started tithing regularly, my finances increased. I live in a better house, and I drive a better car. There is a secret to giving and the secret is increase. God is continually increasing and expanding because He keeps giving, it is His nature.

Chapter Six
HE IS LOVE

I learned that God was love when I was fifteen years old sitting on my bed crying. I was crying because a boy who liked me was moving away. I did not even really like this boy, but he liked me, and I needed that. It was my biggest emotional need as a fifteen-year-old, a super nobody fifteen-year-old.

The world has always been a cold place to me, a place that has never felt safe and never felt warm. I lived in constant fear my entire life. I was so super sensitive that any kind of disapproval whatsoever could start that choking fear that totally shuts me down. I cannot talk. I cannot think. All I want to do is hide and those stupid tears start. I could not control them. I have cried oceans of tears in my lifetime.

No one was safe. No one loved me enough. No one was nice enough, and no one understood the pain and fear inside of me. The only one who came close was my twin sister, Carol. But also, inside of me was this incredible need to be loved. Somehow it culminated in my mind to having a boyfriend. That thought started when I was very young. My mother was pretty and popular, and she was single when I was little and would go on dates.

Mom would sit at the breakfast table when we were very little and tell us about her dates, all her dates and boyfriends. She had been very popular in high school.

Sometimes she would have a date for lunch and another date for supper. She told us one time she was going steady with three boys at the same time. She could not pick between them. Every time she thought she decided which ones she wanted to break up with once she saw him, she would change her mind.

Mom's current dates when we were little would take her to a place called the Stardust. She would dress up pretty and someone in a suit would come to the door and off they would go. It seemed like magic. I had never seen the Stardust, but I had it pictured in my little mind. It was a beautiful place in the clouds that twinkled, and you danced in the sky with a spotlight shining down on you. I could see my mom there in her pretty cocktail dress dancing with a handsome man in a white suit coat a black bow tie and black pants. They would be dancing in the stars all night long. Dates were something like a fairy tale in my mind, like Cinderella. Which was always my all-time favorite fairy tale of all.

As I sat, as a little girl with stars in my eyes listening to my mom talk about dates more than anything I wanted to go on a date. I asked my mom about it, and she assured me, "Oh sure you'll have lots of dates someday."

But I wasn't so sure. Especially in fourth grade when it was time for the carnival. All the boys in class picked a girl to ask her to go with him. Nobody asked me, and I knew why, I was a nobody. Somehow, in my state of nobodiness, I had idolized having a boyfriend to some sort of state of worth. I also had the stupid mistaken notion that in order to have a boyfriend you had to be skinny. I would go for days just eating pickles and coffee.

My sister Carol tells me she snuck and read my diary at about age fifteen. She said she almost died of boredom, and she couldn't even read it. Every day it said, "God, please help me lose weight and give me a boyfriend.

This is where I was when God revealed His love to me. I was a fifteen-year-old emotionally retarded stupid, fearful, worthless mess. And I was sitting on my bed crying like always because some boy I didn't even like was moving away. Oh, yes, the pain was real, it was very real but who on earth would have understood it.

As I was sitting on my bed crying away, and I was a Christian. I had become a Christian the year before, as I was sitting there, God, the Father pulled back the veil. I didn't even know there was a veil until He pulled it back. It was very quick, maybe a second or maybe less, just for an instant I saw Him.

The veil was whatever hides us from the knowledge of His presence. Without the veil, He was there. He was right there with me. I did not see His form I saw His heart. I saw what He was feeling. That brief little moment changed me forever.

He was crying.

He was crying with me.

He was feeling the same pain I was feeling; only His was greater.

He loved me more than I could possibly imagine. There was absolutely no trace of an attitude that I was stupid and immature, and I was. There was only a love that was so strong and so present that He was feeling everything I felt only on a much greater level.

That instant was so quick, but still, I saw His heart and I saw myself in an ocean of His love.

I was in awe.

I immediately stopped crying. I wanted to comfort Him.

52

His pain was greater, even though it was my pain He was carrying.

That moment, that little glimmer of time, had changed my life forever. I knew He loved me so much more than I had ever imagined.

I almost sort of used it against Him, let me explain.

I had such a void inside of me that I was always such a whiny, crying kid. I always complained I was sick; I had a headache or a stomachache. What I really had was a huge void. And I was unable to handle any sort of rejection at all. I was super super sensitive. I walked around in constant emotional pain, afraid of everything and everybody. But even more than rejection I could not even handle responsibility for my own actions. I manipulated my parents by being sick for some emotional comfort.

Now I had a huge source of emotional comfort, God. Once I realized how much He loved me, I made Him hold me constantly. Every time life hurt me which was continually, I held up my arms emotionally and told Him, "You love me, I know You love me." I was like a little toddler who is learning how to walk, they know how to walk but instead they sit down in front of their mommy and hold up their arms and refuse to walk.

I would feel Him, and He would comfort me. He did not pull back the veil, but His love became so real that I ran to Him constantly. And if I did not immediately get picked up when I ran to Him, I pulled on what I perceived to be His weakness, His love for me.

God allowed me to do this for about six or seven years. Then one day it stopped. A woman from church chewed me out at a home meeting and of course I crumpled emotionally. I staggered out of the meeting and got as quickly as I could to my car, so I could get alone with God and have Him hold me.

I managed to blink back the tears as best I could until I got to my car. We were in a house, and I focused on the door and getting out the door and into my car before the heaving sobs came. I ran to the Father as always, but He was not there. He didn't pick me up and I did not feel His love.

I knew He loved me, so I told Him over and over, "I know You love me."

His love is so deep and so intense that I knew it was hurting Him to not come to me. I knew He wanted to hold me, but He didn't, and He wouldn't no matter how much I begged.

Things got worse. Everywhere I went I was getting and facing rejection, and there was no God to pick me up. I could not figure out what was going on. But I just kept pulling on Him for His love.

After a while, maybe a week or two, I don't remember how long anymore. I was going through one of the worse weeks of my life, when something wonderful happened.

God opened the veil again. But this time it was more than an instant. I am not sure if it was five minutes or a half an hour. The veil opened and I was there before Him. Without that veil there it seems like God is an ocean and He just covers everything. His presence is so strong, and it is pure love.

My first feeling and reaction to seeing God, and again it was not His physical appearance it was His heart, I knew what He was feeling, my first reaction was a feeling of belonging. It was like finding out who I was and where I came from. I realized I came from Him, and I was in His image. I was a teeny tiny piece of Him. It was the most intense feeling of coming home and being where I belonged. I never ever wanted to leave.

At first, we just enjoyed each other, loving each other, seeing each other. Then all of a sudden, I realized this was God I was standing in front of, and I needed stuff. We had no money, my husband was facing a felony charge and facing a prison sentence. We needed a lot of help, and this is the Guy to ask for help and face to face even!

I started asking but He stopped me. He told me every need I ever had or will have He has already provided for. It was up to me to take it by faith. His part was done. Then He told me what I suspect was His purpose for our visit all along. He told me He was teaching me to handle rejection. And He reserved the right to no longer carry me but instead He would hold my hand.

To soon the veil began to close. I longed for it to stay open; I wanted to stay there forever. He felt the same way I knew because I knew exactly what He was feeling. He loved being with me. The veil closed.

I learned a few things. This veil is hiding something from us. We are literally standing in an ocean of God's love. He is not far away. You are submerged in Him. He is so in tune with you that He knows your every thought and feels everything you are going through. But He feels it on a deeper level! There is no condemnation or disapproval. He knows, and He understands you completely.

God has all the same emotions that we have. We came from Him. The one thing about Him though is He is not ruled by His emotions, even though He feels them. My time of Him carrying me was over. I had to grow up. It was hard for me, but it was also hard for Him. He was still there but it was different.

God is the source of everything that exists. Everything

that you see or will ever see comes from God. He is the life in everything, even His enemies. He is all powerful, and He is a vast source of energy, light and power. His power is love. He is love and He is light. I believe light and love are connected.

I heard Rick Joyner on YouTube the other day. He was saying He had asked God to be filled with His love. God answered and Rick said he could barely function. He loved everything and everybody. He thought about anyone, and he felt such love for them. He loved everything he saw, the sky, the trees. He was sitting in his car and was even overcome by the steering wheel. It looked so beautiful to him. He said he could barely function, he was so overcome by the beauty of everything.

Although God does not carry me emotionally anymore, I still feel His love. But more importantly whether I feel His love or not, I know it is there.

God is love and we were created to do what He does, love.   *And we have known and believed the love that God has for us, God is love, and he who abides in love abides in God, and God in Him.1John4:16*

Chapter Seven

HE IS JUST

I always wonder why people refuse to believe in hell and they say God is love and He would never send anyone to hell. It is true that God does not want anyone to go to hell we are told that in scripture. But it would be ridiculous to think that God does not punish sin.

We humans on earth punish sin. We do not let murderers and rapists and thieves go unpunished. We have places for them, places called jails and prisons. We do not allow them to continue what they are doing. We even have electric chairs or other means to permanently extinguish murders. We punish those who do evil. We have a system of justice.

If we being unperfected and mortal have a system of justice, how much more does God have a system of justice? God is completely just. God's judgement is completely just and fair. God sees everything. He knows everything. He knows every motive thought and intent of every heart.

Every single one of us sees things differently through our own perspective and bent of our own mind. But God sees things exactly as they really are. This is something we cannot do.

When God looks at us, He can see us completely. Physically He can see us down to the tiniest particle, down to the smallest particle of every atom of your being. His light penetrates and everything within you is laid bare before Him. He also sees every thought and intention of your heart, every word and every action. You are completely laid bare before him.

We can't see what He sees. We justify ourselves in our own minds. We rationalize and tell ourselves we had good reason to do what we did, or what we said. We don't see the real us. It is important for us to ask God to judge our lives now. The results will be painful indeed, but profitable. The fact that God is completely just is so terrifying but at the same time it is so so so good!

Life Seemed Unfair

I struggled with life being unfair and feeling like things were just not fair and never would be. I struggled for years and years. If you have read my others books you already know my story but for those, who haven't I am going to tell it again.

When I was seventeen, I met my husband Jim who had recently been paroled for the second time. I immediately fell in love with him. Jim had been through so much abuse and pain that although he was very broken, his gentle and kind spirit reached out and touched me in a way that no one ever had before.

Emotionally I was locked in a dungeon and Jim seemed to have the key. I was completely and totally smitten with him. I couldn't be without him and followed him everywhere. I was happy when I was with him, I was miserable when I was not.

I could not see why everyone did not want me with him. They saw someone completely different than I did. They knew Jim had too many problems and he was trouble, trouble trouble.

I just knew I could not be without him, so I hung on even though it was unreasonable. I was not a person who operated on reason; I operated on huge inner need. I did know that things were going to be difficult; I just had no idea how difficult they would be.

Jim had no normal, ever. Things were turbulent from the womb. Jim was the fourth and youngest child of a very bad marriage. He was also the second boy. His mother remarried and had another son. Jim fell through the cracks. His mother adored her first son and her youngest son, but she kept Jim locked in the closet.

When I met Jim, he was 27 years old, and he was alone. He had no visitors or letters throughout his years in prison except for toward the end. He had gotten my parents' address from another inmate in prison. Jim had written to them and asked them to write to him because he was lonely. My parents did, they also visited him.

Jim's older brother also spent many years in prison; Jim's mother faithfully visited him and sent him money through the years. That's the way it was. Somehow Jim had fallen through the cracks and Jim was on his own.

When Jim was young Jim was also trouble at school and rarely went. He would wander around the streets of Detroit. He stopped going altogether by ninth grade and was frequently in juvenile hall. From there he graduated to the house of correction and county jails and eventually to prison.

Once Jim landed in prison, he could not seem to stay out long. He kept violating his parole. Jim was not prepared for life whatsoever; he was only prepared for trouble.

At this point we met. Life was never easy again. It was a roller coaster. I had never felt like I belonged on earth anyway, but things got worse. The world became such an unkind place. The person I loved the most in the world was considered the bottom of society. I had to get used to it.

Jim's world consisted of angry police officers, probation officers, lawyers who did not care, condescending judges, and it was for good reason. I felt like we were bugs that needed to be smushed.

Jim tried his hardest. He had to live in a world he wasn't prepared to face as an ex-convict with a ninth-grade education and try to provide for a family feeling as though the whole world hated him. He would do as best as he could, but he would ultimately mess up again and again.

I guess you could call us poor white trash. Even though Jim always worked very hard we never had enough money. We barely ate. When we had a car, it was a junker that barely ran. We never could afford gas or repairs or tires, sometimes it would sit until we could scrape up money for car insurance. We often had to get rides from people. I never had money for the laundry mat, I'd have to use someone's washer, or I never had money for haircuts or new clothes. I looked awful.

I felt like we were worthless. But I didn't mind so much

being worthless to the world as much as I wanted us to be used by God. I wanted to be a saint! I wanted to be great in the Kingdom of Heaven. I wanted Jim and I to be something special somewhere. I longed for some respect, some dignity, some worth. I did not want us always to be at the bottom.

I compensated by trying to be super holy. I read my Bible all day and never watched television. I only read Christian books, and I listened to Christian tapes. I read every book in the church library and listened to every tape. In my mind I was getting holier.

I started looking down on Jim, the holier I was becoming because it seemed he never stopped sinning. I actually thought at that time all my holiness was pleasing to the Lord.

Jim did not share in my quest for holiness. He knew he was a sinner, and his only hope was that somehow, he might make it to heaven. He continually would try to quit drinking and smoking and all his other bad vices but always fail.

He was very humble and would frequently repent at the altar, but he never would even pretend to be holy. He knew better. Even though he felt unworthy he would tell anyone he could about the Lord and would pray with anyone who would to receive Jesus.

It was at this time in my life that the Lord told me that Jim was the one that pleased Him, not me. He was not impressed with my holiness. I was beyond shocked, and asked God why. He then told me Jim was so humble before Him that He would do anything God asked of Him and I was rarely obedient. God also told me Jim had a much higher place in heaven than I did.

Although God told me this stuff, I did not get it. It took

61

years before I understood it. It was totally against my understanding; I mean Christianity is all about being good, right?

I still felt worthless, not just for me but for my whole family. We frequently had chaos. And I kept thinking this miracle was going to happen and God was going to use us in some miraculous way that would show everyone that we weren't worthless.

I mean if the whole body of Christ were in the condition, we were in it would not be good. Not that we weren't improving a little, we were, but years were going by, and we had no great works to show for our life. We were still quite a mess.

I would see other Christians making such a difference and realize we were just on the bottom, especially Jim. I wanted someone, someday, to see the good in him. Life did not seem fair, somehow, we seemed born to be worthless no matter what.

My whole life changed the day I read *The Final Quest.* In the book the author, Rick Joyner has a vision of two different men. The one is a devoted Christian who is zealously serving the Lord and helping people, the other is a bum. He sees the bum walking down an alley and a cat gets in his way. He is about to kick the cat but instead he just shoves it out of his way with his foot, rather gruffly.

God asks Rick which of the two men pleases Him more and of course Rick answers the Christian. But to Rick's complete surprise God says the bum pleases Him more. Then God explains to Rick the Christian man was raised in a loving home. He went to a good Bible school and God had given him one hundred shares of love of which he was using seventy-five.

Next God told Rick about the bum; he was born deaf. His parents abused him and kept him locked in the attic. Later the authorities find him and put him in an institution where the abuse continues. As an adult he is turned out on the street and homeless. Then God explains he, the bum, is full of rage but to overcome the rage God has given the bum three shares of love of which he used all three not to kick the cat!

At this point as I was reading this book, I finally understood! I finally understood that God is so just! I finally understood that we weren't being judged by God by where we were in life but by how hard we were trying and how much of His love we were using to overcome. I finally realized my husband was like this bum, he was very pleasing to God because he was using everything he had!

We were not worthless, even if only God understood this, that was fine by me, we were not worthless.

I remember I was reading the book in my bedroom on my bed. The next thing I knew I was running around the house I was laughing; I was crying all at the same time. Then I was on my knees on the living room floor.

"God, You are so just! You are so just!" I kept crying. I could not contain my joy. I finally understood what God had been trying to tell me for years.

God is so just it amazes me; it absolutely amazes me!!!!!!

I keep learning that the more I find out about God the better it gets. He is good, He is just so good! You see, He knows all the hurt and rage that some people carry because of all the abuse that has been done to them, and then he sees that effort they put forth against all that pain, to love maybe even a cat. And the world stands by and sees only a bum, but God sees victory, God is pleased. So pleased that He gives them a higher place in heaven.

It is not about what we see, it is about what He sees. We are incapable of judging others or even ourselves. He sees everything and He is the only one who sees everything, and He is totally and completely just.

Chapter Eight

"HE SCARES ME BUT I LIKE IT"

{The Fear of the Lord}

"And do not fear those who kill the body but cannot kill the soul. But rather fear Him who is able to destroy both soul and body in hell." Matthew 10:28

I talked about in the beginning of the book how I felt like I had God in my pocket, because He was so nice. That is because God had made Himself very small to reach me. He had only revealed to me a very small part of Himself. I have since learned that God is so huge and so powerful that He is terrifying. I was absolutely ridiculous to think I was some kind of expert on God. I heard a saying once and I think that it is true. *To the baby Christian, Jesus is the Lamb, to the young Christian He is the Lion and to the mature Christian He is both, the Lion and the Lamb.*

I remember when my daughter Joy was about eight or nine years old. We were praying together, and God spoke prophetically to her through me. Only it was not me; it was one of those moments when I heard my voice speaking but I was as surprised at what was coming out of my mouth as she was. Even my voice did not sound like normal; it almost seemed as if there were thunder in it.

The presence of God was overpowering as He spoke to Joy, I was trembling. God was not speaking to her as one would speak to a little girl. He was speaking to her like a seasoned warrior. Joy had been saved at the age of two and by nine she was a mature believer.

God was speaking powerfully over Joy's life. He was telling her He had called her to be a great warrior in His kingdom. He was speaking to her of her future, and what He was saying seemed like a dream. It was also a firm word calling her to obedience. His voice seemed like a roar that was vibrating through my body. Both Joy and I trembled in His presence.

After He was done speaking Joy kept saying over and over, "He scares me, but I like it."

It was scary, I had to agree, but I liked it too. God was getting bigger to me and as He got bigger, I was realizing He was so much more than I had thought He was.

Too Much of God?

I would like to tell you about the most intense

experience I have ever had with God so far in my life. I know I have mentioned it several times in previous books, but I need to tell it again because it was my first real experience with the fear of the Lord.

I am one that can never get enough of God. I get God cravings. I get restlessness and a yearning for more of Him. One night about sixteen years ago I had a day off from work, so I decided I was going to worship God all night long. Everyone was in bed except my son Jay who was away for the night, so I loaded up my CD player with seven worship CDs.

Well, I didn't make it very long, I fell asleep. But I awoke in the middle of the night to the presence of God. This was not like anything I had ever experienced before. It was very uncomfortable.

Part of me was thinking that this is great, God is here, but I really and truly felt like I was going to die. This was not like when The Father pulled back the veil and we were communicating heart to heart. This was a penetrating presence that was illuminating everything in me. It was like all the words I have said and all the things I had watched on television and all my thoughts were right there. They were not in the past, they were there. And they were so vile in His light. He was pure and penetrating and holy. I was doing some serious repenting.

I told God that I loved being in His presence, but I needed Him to tone it down or I was going to die. I was still aware of being in my living room but being in my living room was not my reality, God's presence was. I could not move my body or speak; I spoke to the Lord in my head. My body was jerking violently on the floor.

God did not speak. But His presence was holy, and I was aware of how foul my words and thoughts and deeds were next to Him. I laid there for hours and when my son, Jay, came in early in the morning I tried to speak to him but couldn't. I managed to sputter, "GOD!"

Jay cried, "I feel Him too," and fell on the floor and started sobbing.

I realized that no one could stand before God without the blood of Jesus; it would be too terrifying and even with it was terrifying.

The Terror of the Lord

John Paul Jackson, the prophet, had an experience that makes mine seem pale. His exact words were, "it scared the stuffings out of me."

He was whisked into the Throne Room of God and found himself standing before the Throne. He was so close to God's Throne the seven lampstands were actually behind him. John Paul said he was terrified! He stood there screaming. All he could do was scream in terror. He also felt like he was going to die, he said He felt like God was going to kill him and whatever the reason he knew it was right.[I could relate to that}

Standing there in that extreme light John Paul's awareness was heightened as the light coursed through his body he said that he was aware of every single particle of his body, cellular and sub cellular and structures that science hasn't even discovered yet.

John Paul says he saw the Throne and the rings of light around it and the angels encircling the throne crying, "Holy, holy, holy!" John Paul describes it like being at the nucleus of an atom with the angels spinning around the throne. There was constant motion and great noise.

He witnessed lights of every shape, size, and color rocketing out of the Light of the Father and ripping through the atmosphere with great sound and intensity at a rate of billions per second, which he perceived with his heightened awareness.

He saw lightning's and balls of light of every color size and shape continually, constantly at unbelievable speed exploding forth from the throne and with each an angel would cry out, "holy!" John heard that constant cry from the angels in machine gun speed as the angels were witnessing the mighty acts of God.

Only with his heightened awareness could he distinguish the billions of cries from the angels as they cried out "holy" at each burst of light proceeded from the Father. He said the rapid cries from the angels blended together and sounded like thunder. John Paul realized as he was seeing, these lights of every shape size and color shooting forth, billions per second, that it was God reacting with His creation. John Paul was overcome with awe and terror.

Although it was a turning point in John Paul's life and many of his best teachings came from the things he learned and experienced standing there, he was so terrified it took him a few years to get willing to revisit it. Just hearing John Paul talk about it on his many YouTube sermons fills me with awe and a sense of wonder about this marvelous place.

John Paul said during this time he saw people throw themselves into the abyss to flee from God's presence. God did not throw them in, they threw themselves in. His holiness is absolutely terrifying to those who choose darkness.

This reminds me of a passage of Revelation.

Then the sky receded as a scroll when it is rolled up, and every mountain and island was moved out of its place. And the kings of the earth, the great men, the rich men, the commanders, the mighty men, every slave and every free man, hid themselves in the caves and in the rocks of the mountains, and said to the mountains and rocks, "fall on us and hide us from the face of Him who sits on the throne and from the wrath of the lamb!" Revelation 6:14-16

Healthy Fear

We need to have a balance of our understanding of God. He has extended to us His love and mercy and that is an awesome thing, but we should respect Him and the price that it cost Him. And we should also realize the magnitude of who He is and not presume upon His grace.

Satan and all his hordes of evil doers despise us because of this grace that has been offered to us and not to them. They goad us to disregard the things that are holy and treat them lightly, and they want us to believe that because God does not immediately punish sin that we can live and speak any way we want to. But they fear Him. They fear the Lord and His light is torment to them.

To fear the Lord is not bad, it is healthy, and it is wisdom. I have begun to fear the Lord when I realize the magnitude of His power, His might and His penetrating light. God sees and hears every thought word and action I have ever committed, and He hears them all simultaneously because He dwells on the past present and future all at the same time.

There is nothing I can hide from Him. I do not need to run from Him though, I need to be obedient and repentant and allow His Spirit to work in me. I need to take seriously the things He takes seriously. I will end this chapter with some of the verses on the fear of the Lord.

The fear of the Lord is the beginning of wisdom; A good understanding have all who do His commandments. Psalm111:10

Blessed is the man who fears the Lord, who delights greatly in His commandments. Psalm 112:1

The fear of the Lord prolongs days, But the years of the wicked will be shortened. Proverbs 10:27

The fear of the Lord leads to life, and he who has it will abide in satisfaction; he will not be visited with evil. Proverbs 19:23

Behold the eye of the Lord is on those who fear Him, on those who hope in His mercy, to deliver their soul from death and to keep them alive in famine. Psalm 33:18-19

The angel of the Lord encamps around those who fear Him and delivers them. Psalm 34:7

Who is the man that fears the Lord? Him shall He teach in the way He chooses. Psalm 25:12

You have given a banner to those who fear You, that it may be displayed because of truth Psalm 60:4

In the fear of the Lord there is strong confidence, and His children will have a place of refuge. The fear of the Lord is a fountain of life, to turn one away from the snares of death. Proverbs 14:26-27

Chapter Nine

INSIDE OF GOD, THE HEART OF THE FATHER

This topic is so exciting to me that it takes my breath away. What is inside of God? We get a glimpse in the book of Ezekiel, in all places in a text about Lucifer.

You were the anointed cherub who covers;

I established you;

You were on the holy mountain of God;

You walked back and forth in the midst of the fiery stones.

You were perfect in your ways from the day you were created,

Till iniquity was found in you. Ezekiel 28:14-15

Lucifer may have been the highest angel. He was actually allowed to enter into the heart of the Father. The heart of the Father is described as fiery stones. This is a very holy place and Lucifer was able to go there. He went in and out of the heart of the Father, a huge and holy honor. Eventually he was kicked out not only from within the Father but also out of heaven.

So just what are these fiery stones all about? Kat Kerr in her second book *Revealing Heaven2* describes being caught up to the throne of the Father. While she was there, He reached into Himself and pulled out the largest diamond she has ever seen. She also described a blue fire burning around the stone and as she watched a rainbow also formed around it. She realized the magnificent rainbow around the throne of God was coming from the fiery stones within Him.

If this sounds unusual to you, to have stones inside, just remember we are described in the book of Peter as a living stone.

Coming to Him as a living stone, rejected indeed by men, but chosen by God and precious, You also as living stones, are being built up a spiritual house, a holy priesthood, to offer up spiritual sacrifices acceptable to God through Jesus Christ. 1 Peter2:4-5

In one of her sermons Kat Kerr said that when we come to the Lord, then Father places a burning stone from within Himself inside of us. So, we literally carry a part of His heart within us!

Anna Rountree, in her book, *The Heavens Opened*, describes actually entering the Father, with Jesus at her side, and standing among the stones of fire within the heart of the Father.

We were standing amid the coals that were white from intense heat. I too began to heat up. The light was so

bright that I could barely see Jesus for the glory within the blazing, white haze.

Suddenly Jesus was standing in front of me within the coals of fire. Brilliant white light was coming from Him; tongues of fire radiated out from Him at intervals. His eyes were aflame also. He spoke, "As my heart is represented by the garden in paradise, each believer's heart is likewise represented as a locked garden wherein we meet. The Father's heart is represented by these coals of fire, aflame with love. The Father's heart is pure, aflame and holy. You must be invited to walk amid the coals of fire, for although our Father loves all, not all are invited within.

The fiery stones within the heart of the Father is a place where some but not all will be invited. I would love to be invited into the heart of the Father.

The River of Life

So within the heart of God is the fiery stones, but there is more there also because out of the Father flows the River of Life. The River of Life, which is the river that flows throughout heaven is filled with gemstones. These beautiful stones also have their origin from God. They are everywhere in heaven. We are told the origination point of this river is from the Father.

And the water of this River brings life and healing to those who enter. This water is pure love, and it heals all who enter it. Those who are coming to heaven from earth carrying the trauma to their souls from earth life, come first to this River for cleansing, to begin their new existence in heaven, free from the cares of this fallen world. This is where the angels and their loves ones lead them first, on entrance to paradise.

Neville Johnson, a wonderful minister of the gospel from Australia, tells in his visits to heaven of seeing people in this River. One man that Neville noticed had been saved but he had killed several people and he spent quite a bit of time in this marvelous River before moving on into deeper parts of heaven. He had made it to heaven, but his soul was very damaged because of the deep sin he had come from. Neville says some spend days in the river.

The water from the river is described as delightful. Those who enter find they can breathe underwater and talk. One woman who wrote about an experience there said it washed the cobwebs from her mind. The River of Life prepares us for the divine life.

We also are told we have rivers of living water flowing out of our bellies. {John 7:38] Again we resemble the Father. But there is more to the heart of the Father.

The Ancient Paths

Within the heart of God was our dwelling place, the ancient paths. Within the heart of God is a beautiful place where we existed, as spirits, within him, long before the world was created. He foreknew us. We have actually been around a very long time. Our spirits were inside of the Father, we lived inside of Him.

I have heard many different people who have actually visited the throne describe these spirits, us. Kat Kerr says in her book, when she is caught up before the Throne and standing before the Father, she has seen little spirits flowing in and out of the glory flowing from His being and they are saying, "Send me, please send me." They want to be sent to earth. She adds they do not have a real body so that cannot exist outside of the Father.

Neville Johnson has mentioned seeing these little spirits also in the glory of the Father and hearing them say, "Please send me, I want to be a redeemed spirt, please send me."

Jesse Duplantis in his book, *Heaven, Close Encounters of the God Kind,* he describes seeing these little spirits also.

I saw new lives of little babies singing and flying around God's Throne. It seemed to me that babies just came out of the breath of God. They looked like they were wearing little nightgowns. They flew into the presence of Jehovah.

I realized they were new souls who came from the thoughts of God. God thinks kids. Now I know why these newborn babies are so precious. Babies are gifts given to us directly from the throne of God.

I heard them saying to God, "Can I be a spirit? Would you send me to earth so I can be a spirit? I want to be a redeemed person. Can I be a spirit?"

Our home for a very long time was the ancient paths within the heart of God. We existed there. Kat Kerr says we played there. It is a world within the heart of God which is very beautiful.

While we were inside of God, He created the physical plane for us. He created the earth for us. And when He sends us to earth, we become a tri-part being. He knits our spirit into our body at the moment of conception. And we become a person who can exist on earth in the physical realm but also in the spiritual realm. {If we are born again}

"Summer Needs Help"

My daughter Joy had a conversation with God about her existence before she was born. In her life within God, He told her that she was always helping everyone, whether they needed it or not. That is just how she is. He said I sent you to Summer, your mother, because she needed help.

It is true, I really needed help. I always felt like I was just hanging on by my fingernails. She is the kid that helped me the most and she started very young. I remember when she was just a baby. I drove a large van and I would put her car seat on the floor next to the driver's seat. She was only a couple months old, and she would have her face fixed on mine and she would be smiling at me. I would feel peace pouring off of her. She seemed like she was born to help me.

When she was seven years old, I started running a paper route, delivering close to 500 papers per night. I did it for three and a half years seven days a week including Christmas, and Joy would wake herself up and go with me. She didn't want me to go alone. Often, she would work like a grown-up. Somehow, she remembered her mission.

Sometimes small children have memory of the world inside of God, Neville Johnson retells of his wife hearing a conversation between two very small children. One said to the other, "Remember what it was like before we came here. The colors were much brighter, and the trees were so beautiful."

Soon these memories fade.

I believe we had a life there, some danced some sang

some painted. Somehow child prodigies hung onto their talents and still have them. There is a young lady, named Akiane Kramarik who at four years old began to paint heavenly scenes in magnificent colors and she also paints beautiful pictures of Jesus. I believe the answer to this mystery has to do with her life in the heart of God, in the ancient paths where we existed in His heart. She is painting the places she has been.

We used to exist in the Father's heart. Now He has a place in ours. I have heard it said that the very same part of the Father's heart that we existed is where He now exists in our hearts. That is because we are created in His image, and for Him.

There is nowhere that God does not exist but there is yet another world inside of our Father. We have little glimpses of what is there, stones of fire, a River of Life and a world where we lived inside of Him before He sent us to earth. The heart of the Father is a very special place for us. It was the beginning of our existence; it was our home.

Chapter Ten

THE GARDEN, THE HEART OF JESUS

We read in the last chapter, a passage from Anna Rountree in which Jesus explained to her that His heart was represented by the Garden and likewise our hearts are also represented by a garden. {**"As my heart is represented by the garden in paradise, each believer's heart is likewise represented as a locked garden where we meet."**} We will look into this in this chapter.

When God made Adam and Eve, He made them for Himself in His image. We are made for intimacy with God. God placed Adam and Eve in the Garden of Eden. In the middle of the Garden grew the Tree of Life. God would come and walk in the Garden in the cool of the day. This was the place of intimacy with man, the Garden of the Lord.

In heaven this Garden still exists. Anna Rountree visited this Garden. At the entrance the Cherubim still stood singing praise to God. In order to enter the Garden, she passed under their outstretched wings. Everything in the Garden, all the beautiful flowering plants, reflected Christ. She felt His presence there. There was even the sound of music coming from everything in the Garden. It was sweet music from the heart of Jesus to the Father. The angel that accompanied her explained that this was Jesus' Garden and He walked there.

In the middle of the Garden, she saw a large tree that was so bright and had so much light coming from it that it was not the color of a tree on earth. It was laden with fruit. It was the Tree of Life.

A Garden Within Us

Just as the heart of Jesus is represented as a Garden, so is our heart. In the midst of each one of us is a place of intimacy, which is created for fellowship with Jesus. It is also a Garden.

I believe the writer, C Austin Miles, of the hymn, I Come to the Garden Alone, written in the year, 1912, had a revelation of this place of intimacy with Christ.

I come to the garden alone,
While the dew is still on the roses,
And the voice I hear falling on my ear,
The Son of God discloses,
And He walks with me and He talks with me
And He tells me I am His own

And the joy we share as we tarry there,
None other has ever none.

This song is about a real place in the heart of every believer. Anna Rountree also writes in her first book about walking with the Lord in her garden. She found herself with the Lord in a garden she said it was a private garden and not extremely large but large enough to have several trees planted a three-tiered fountain in the center a path around it and a large apricot tree with a bench for two underneath. I will quote her book,

The path circled the garden, with plantings near the wall as well as on the opposite side of the path in the center of the garden. Camphire {henna} was blooming there, and the star of Bethlehem, blue flax and scarlet lily were blooming in beds near it.

"Who tends this garden?" I asked.

"You do, "He answered.

"I tend this garden?" I exclaimed with astonishment.

"Yes," He replied.

I looked over the garden. I felt that I had been here before, but the feeling was an elusive impression, rather like trying to piece together a dream when you only remember snatches of it. I could not bring it into clear focus.

"Would you tell me of this garden, Lord?" I asked finally.

"Each garden is different. Each is unique, and I delight in each." He paused before speaking again. "Do you enjoy being here?" He asked.

"Yes, it's…." I could not find the words.

"Yes, "He agreed.

We came to a spring that flowed from a rock in the garden. Spanning the water was an arch of a bridge that seemed only wide enough for two people. As I thought about it the bench near the fountain also only seemed wide enough for two. Perhaps this was a garden for lovers.

Before Jesus leaves Anna, He gives her a golden key on a scarlet cord that unlocks the gate to the garden. He tells her whenever she wishes she may unlock the gate and He will meet her there.

We have been created for intimacy with God. And God has even created in our hearts a special place for that intimacy. In the image of Jesus, Our Savior, Our Creator, Our Lord, we have a special place in our hearts made for fellowship with Him. It is a garden.

Awake, O north wind,
And come, O south!
Blow upon my garden,
That its spices may flow out,
Let my beloved come to his garden
And eat its pleasant fruits.
Song of Solomon 4:16

Neville Johnson also has insight on this subject; he talks about it in his online message called the Garden of God. He tells how Jesus brought him into a beautiful garden in paradise. He also saw beautiful fountains and ponds with fish. He tells how beautiful the aromas of the garden were and how lovely the plants were. He called it other worldly and heavenly.

Jesus then told Neville, "Tell my people, when I can walk in your garden, then you can walk in Mine."

Our garden has to do with intimacy with Jesus,

but it is also more than that. It has to do with developing the fruit of the spirit in our life. The fruit of the spirit are listed in Galatians 5:22-23. They are love, joy, peace, patience, kindness, goodness and faithfulness, gentleness and self-control.

A Beautiful Smell

Neville also teaches how each of these attributes when manifested in our lives has a color and a beautiful smell in the spirit realm. Such as thankfulness has a red color, and a wonderful smell and love is a bright white light but contains all the colors of the rainbow. Our garden is a manifestation of the fruit of the spirit in our lives. It is very apparent in the spirit realm. And of course, the opposite is true, the works of the flesh such as anger, greed or jealousy, emit a dark ugly color or light and a putrid smell.

Song of Solomon 4:14 is talking about our inner garden. It lists nine plants that correlate with the nine fruits of the spirit.

You are a garden locked up my sister my bride; you are a spring enclosed, a sealed fountain. Your plants are an orchard of pomegranates with choice fruits, with henna and nard, nard and saffron, calamus and cinnamon, with every kind of incense tree {frankincense], with myrrh and aloes and all the finest spices. Song of Solomon 4:12-14

All of these plants are known for their exquisite aromas and beautiful flowers. All of them but cinnamon are used in perfumes and are costly. This was quite a delightful garden. When we tend out inner garden and allow the fruit of the spirit to be formed within us, we become very beautiful inside. We carry the most beautiful blend of aromas. We become a garden that is delightful.

One night not too long ago I woke up in the night to the most beautiful smell. In fact, I believe it was the smell that woke me up. I believe the smell was all the aromas listed in Song of Solomon, I know I could smell the cinnamon and the frankincense. I didn't just get a faint whiff; I sniffed in and just enjoyed the strong beautiful aroma. I believe it was Jesus. After a few minutes the smell was gone and I went back to sleep, feeling excited knowing the Lord had been present.

One of the most delightful parts of gardens is the beautiful smells. As we tend our garden we will begin to smell like Jesus.

Jesus said that when He can walk in our garden then we can walk in His. We can enter His realm. We can find Him. We can visit paradise.

I want to visit paradise. I want to walk in the Garden of Jesus.

The fruit of the spirit does not develop through taking the easy way in life. It takes work to tend the garden in our hearts and develop the fruits of the spirit, but it is worth it because when Jesus can walk in our garden then we can walk in His.

Chapter Eleven

WHO WAS AND IS AND IS TO COME

And the four living creatures, each having six wings, were full of eyes around and within. And they do not rest day or night, saying: "Holy, holy, holy, Lord God Almighty, Who was and is and is to come!"

God is present in the present, the past and the future all at the same time. He is outside of time. He exists in the past, present and future simultaneously. He is with you right now in your past, in the present and in your future. You are in Him. You exist in Him.

When I figured out what that means, I asked God if I could talk to my future self, and He let me. I had to know if things ever get better and according to her, {me} they do.

She, {I} told me, "You think that things will never change," {and she was right} and then she told me, "But they do." She did not seem like me at all, she seemed so happy. Then she told me something that really surprised me, she told me to enjoy every moment of my life, even the bad ones! Boy, does she know me! I have been holding my breath my whole life just waiting to get to heaven so I can enjoy myself. Earth is something to be endured, not enjoyed. I have been trying to work on that. She knows me because I am her and I rarely enjoy the good moments, life is too heavy, and she wants me to even enjoy the bad moments?

God told me one time that when He sees me, He sees my whole life not just the present. That is kind of mind bending because we are eternal, and our life never ends. But the point is, God sees you ten thousand years from now, in fact you are there with Him.

So, the things He is doing in your life right now that you do not understand, it is because He is preparing you for then. He is trying to promote you. It may seem really hard, but He is really doing what is best.

Different things are important from that perspective, and it is not money or a new shed for your backyard. {I have been trying to get a new shed for my back yard}. God is getting you ready for then, {eternity]

Your life on earth determines your place in eternity. How you live is very important! This stuff really is in the Bible I have just always read right over it and ignored it.

Beloved, do not think it strange concerning the fiery trial, which is to try you, as though some strange thing happened to you; But rejoice to the extent that you partake of Christ's sufferings that when His glory is revealed, you may be glad with exceeding joy. 1 Peter 4:12-13

Sufferings do not seem like something to rejoice about

if we only see the now. But they are a very small price to pay from an eternal perspective, if you could see the glory that is to come.

We do not have that perspective, but God does. For that reason, we need to trust His perspective and ask Him who sees the future:

"Where do You want me to go?"

"What do You want me to do?"

"What is Your plan for my life?"

Have you ever been driving along through traffic, and something is going on in the other lane, heading the opposite direction? It is stopped up for miles. And as you drive the other way, and you see people heading into that mess you wish you had a sign you could hold up to say turn around. I have thought of that many times. You don't want them to get caught in that mess. You know what is ahead and they don't.

God knows what is ahead of you every single day. In fact, before the world began, He knew what would happen to you today. We need to come to Him and get the low down from someone who can see ahead of us. He has the big picture.

I hope while you are reading this you feel something starting to shift, your trust. Our trust needs to be in the God, who was and is and is to come. He has the perspective that we don't have, He knows what is coming today, tomorrow, next year, in ten years in twenty years in a hundred years and in a thousand years, because He is there right now, and so are you in Him.

Time travel is totally exciting to me. It is not just science fiction. God takes people to the past and the future. God took Moses to the past and he wrote the story of creation in Genesis. God took John into the future, and He wrote

Revelation. There are people God is doing the same with now. John Paul Jackson was taken to the past, he talks about it in His sermon called, *The God of Time and Space.* Neville Johnson in several of his sermons tells of seeing into the Millennium. One of his sermons he talks about is called *The Big Picture.*

When we get inner healing, in God we go into the past with God, who is already there. God is there with us and can restore the hurts that happened in the past.

I have heard Bruce Allen, a minister who walks in the powers of the age to come, explain that when light travels it is present along the whole path it travels. It is still present at point A and at point B. Therefore, we all exist in light and the past still exists. {At least I think that is what he was trying to say, it is a little above me}.

We are created in God's image, and we exist in God who is outside of time. The bounds of time should no longer hold us down. We need to become more focused on eternal things, the things that do not pass away. I wrote about this in my book, *What Can I Do for God?*

We existed inside of God before the foundation of the world {Ephesians 1:4} We exist in God in the eons to come. We need to exist in God right now. We need to move right into Him.

The Mountain

I recently had a magnificent dream. I dreamt I was driving down the road with my sister and brother-in-law and we drove into a tunnel. The tunnel led to the inside of a huge mountain.

As we drove in, I felt an exhilaration. The walls were so

thick and strong, thick walls of stone from the sides of the mountain. I saw a grocery store in there and I thought, "I want to shop here!" I was so thrilled to be in this mountain and I wanted the map so I could come there again.

I thought of my grandson who loves rocks and nature and I wanted to show him the inside of this mountain. I started asking people in the mountain where it was, what road it was on and how to get there. I never got a straight answer, but they had a little look in their eye that made me realize they were not giving me that answer for a reason.

There were beautiful rooms in the mountain, and one had a skylight that looked up through the mountain high into the sky. As I looked up, I saw thick dark clouds that also made me tremble with excitement. Inside the mountain I had such a feeling of wonder and peace and awe. It was a strong sense of God's presence. I wanted to be able to keep going there and I wanted to bring my grandson.

The whole next day I had such a marvelous feeling, every time I thought of the dream. I wanted to know what it meant.

Well, I figured out that the mountain was being in God, that safe place of His presence that is impenetrable and full of wonder. The clouds were the cloud of His presence. The entrance I finally realized was faith. {My sister and brother-in-law are Rhema graduates; they stand for faith.}

The people in the mountain were angels {they had that knowing look.} And my grandson stood for you, my readers, those whom I want to unveil the wonder of God to.

The dream has remained with me. When I close my eyes and pray, I can enter the mountain again by faith and feel that wonderful feeling that is from another world. It is a heavenly feeling of awe and wonder, peace and love and safety and everything good. It is a feeling of being within God Himself.

I want to take you there. I want to show you that place. It is indescribable in wonder and awe and majesty. It is so desirable to be there. It is being within God Himself. I want you to be able to find the entrance too and go there at will. It is an eternal place. God has forever existed and in Him is eternity. This is where you came from, this eternal place; you have actually come from inside of the heart of God.

Volume 2
LET'S TALK ABOUT US

Chapter Twelve

WHO AM I?

Here we are on this planet, lots of us. We have to figure out what life is about, why are we here? We can look around and we see plants and animals, the world has beautiful places. We see the sun rise in the morning, every morning and we see it set in the evening. We see beautiful flowers growing and trees. There are things for us to eat here, delicious things. Everything we need to live is provided for us here.

We look around and see the planet we are living on, and it is a place of wonder. There is so much around us to see and experience. Then at night when it is dark, we can look up at the sky and see millions and billions of stars and we realize how vast the universe is and it creates in us an awe. Who am I? What am I? Why am I here?

Now we learn from the adults around us, but really, they have not been here very long either, and they learned from the adults around them also, so most of the knowledge we have is told to us. Somewhere at some time, someone really smart figured things out. We have homes that keep us warm with lights and power and water and heat. Someone figured out telephones and automobiles and airplanes and many other things. But who is in charge here?

For a long time, our parents are in charge of us, we do what they tell us too, or get spanked. {At least in my day we got spanked] They learned from their parents. Some of us remember our grandparents, some of us may even remember our great grandparents, but we lose track of things before that. We are from a long line of people, but we don't know too much about them. I know back as far as my grandmother and grandfather on my mother's side. They were both born in the 1890's. I know my grandmother's parents' names but little about them. I know less about grandpa's side. Who were the people before my grandparents?

How long have I existed? I was born in 1961 but I do not remember too much about life until I was a little older. It is hazy. In fact, I forget a lot of things. I read old diaries and read things I wrote but have no memory of.

Somewhere along the line I learned about death. What I learned is that a person I love, such as Grandpa dies and disappears, and I never see him again. And then there is something equally as fascinating and that is birth. I learned about birth when I had children because I hadn't been around babies.

This little boy was born, and I really did not have that

much to do with it. He was formed in my womb, but I did not create him. It was as much of a surprise to me when he was born as anyone. I wondered what he would be like, I did not even know if he were a he or a she.

I noticed he had his personality even before he was born. He would get grumpy with me when I skipped a meal. I was not a regular eater, I would sometimes skip several meals, and that did not work when I got pregnant. He would kick and kick when I skipped a meal. He is thirty-five years old now and he still gets grouchy when he is hungry.

This wonderful person was formed inside me; he came out perfect with ten fingers and ten toes. I live in a world of wonder. Something amazing happened a child developed on the inside of me, I gave birth and now I have this son to raise.

We have scientists that study about everything and they can give us some answers but really there is so much they do not know. How do we get answers? How do find out about the world? How do we find out about ourselves? How do we know God is real?

?? ?????????????????????????????

Well, it is in us. It is just in us, especially when we were children. We came here with a purpose, and it is in us. Jesus came to earth with a purpose. He knew His purpose before He came. Whether He remembered His purpose or rediscovered His purpose, I don't know, but it was placed inside of Him, from before He came.

We have come here with a purpose. We asked to come here. Our purpose is placed inside of us. We have the opportunity to develop more of God in us. Like Jesus we have a divine destiny for each of our lives, and that is why we have come.

Many times, children have more of an understanding of God because their purpose has faded less from their memory.

I was worried my daughter's children were not learning enough about God. She was in an abusive marriage and over her head. Her kids were not getting the biblical training I felt they needed. They were small, 4,3 and 1 year old. But their mother was a seasoned believer by the age of four; I wanted the same for them.

One day we were all at the lake swimming, not just my daughter Joy and her three but my son and his two children also. There were also some teenagers at the beach whom I only briefly noticed.

Suddenly one of the teenagers dragged his friend up on the beach, he had drowned. My son Jay rounded up all the kids and brought them away from the beach so they would not be traumatized by the drowned young man. Joy and I were caught up with trying to revive the young man. We were doing CPR and praying for him, well sort of. I hollered "Jesus" over and over between every breath I gave him. We did not see David, the four-year-old was standing there watching the whole thing.

Soon the paramedics came and shooed us away and we did not learn until later the young man had died. I wondered what the affect it would have on a four-year-old. I wondered how we would explain the meaning of death to him.

That night when Joy was putting David to bed he said to his mother, "Mommy that boy died."

"Yes, "Joy responded.

"Mommy, I want to pray," he said.

David gave his heart to the Lord that night. It was all his

idea. He understood what he saw, and he realized he needed a Savior. I was amazed, utterly amazed.

Yes, we find ourselves here on this planet and God's presence is veiled from our eyes but, His spirit is drawing us. Many times, children in their innocence are extremely sensitive to God. He is present here with us. The knowledge of God has been placed within us.

Neville Johnson, whom I will keep mentioning because his teaching is so amazing, he says that God gives every human being a chance to accept Him. He says that those who have never heard the gospel will still have the choice to receive the Lord. He visits every soul, at some point in their life or at their death.

I know He came to me. He visited me personally and let me know He loved me. I have recently heard of amazing stories of Jesus visiting people of other religions in their dreams. God's spirit will deal with each and every spirit He has created. Some will receive Him, and some will reject Him.

We have not been left alone on this planet. Every person is assigned angels at their birth. The spirit of God hovers over each person during their life and each person on earth. God is constantly drawing us unto Himself.

I have found that every person in my life, who has told me that they do not believe in God, really do. They are just angry with Him. They blame Him for some evil, or disappointment and they get even by saying He doesn't exist.

I am finding the older I become, that the God I do not see is becoming more real than this world that I do.

No, we are not alone on this beautiful planet. All light and life come from God. We are standing in Him we exist in Him. The whole universe exists in Him. This thing called life that is in us, is His breath within us. He breathed and we lived. God is close, God is very close. He is as close as your beating heart and your every thought. We have come here for a purpose.

For the wrath of God is revealed from heaven against all ungodliness and unrighteousness of men, who suppress the truth in unrighteousness, because what may be known of God is manifest in them, for God has shown it to them. For since the creation of the world His invisible attributes are clearly seen, being understood by the things that are made, even His eternal power and Godhead so that they are without excuse, Romans 1:18-20

Chapter Thirteen
CREATED IN HIS IMAGE

Then God said, "Let Us make man in Our image,
according to Our likeness, Genesis 1:26a

Katt Kerr, an amazing woman who has been taken to heaven multiple times and shown many wonderful things, teaches a good teaching on being created in God's image. The Lord showed her how each of the three parts of our being is created in the likeness of each of the three parts of God's being. That makes sense. We were created by all three parts of the Trinity, and we are created in each of Their images.

The Father

Our Spirit is created in the image of the Father. The Father is a spirit, and so are we. And it is the spirit part of our being that came from the Father and communes with the

Father. He speaks to our spirit; rarely does he speak to us in an audible voice that our mind or our physical ears can hear. {When He does believe me, you will know because His voice is like thunder.} But I am not quite as in tune to hearing with my spirit as I am with my ears. Our spirits have lived for eons in the heart of the Father, and our spirit man resembles Him.

We were created to love like He loves. And who do we love to love but our own offspring. When we become parents, we become more like the Father. I have noticed many playboys settle down when they become parents. They love their children so much the worldly life becomes unappealing. Many men and women return to church after becoming parents. They love their children and want them to be raised properly.

The Father loves us in a way we cannot imagine. Everything that God does in our lives is redemptive. Everything He does comes from one motivation and that is love, real love. He does what is best for us. God cannot respond any other way but out of love because it would be against His nature. This is something you can totally base your life upon. You can trust God totally and know He will redeem every situation you find yourself in if you have given Him that place in your life.

Not that you will not be tested, believe me you will be tested. If you chose to totally trust God, you will be tested. If you refuse to believe anything except that God is good and continue to trust Him no matter what your circumstances are telling you, then you will be an overcomer in this life and in a place that although Satan will try to destroy you. He will not be able to though, because there will be nothing, he can do to you that will cause you to stop trusting God.

Many people do not understand this truth, that God is love, and have an image of God as an angry judgmental character with a big hammer waiting to squash them. Sometimes this is because that is the way their earthly father treated them, and they think God is the same. Or sometimes it is because they do not understand the reason bad things happen and they blame everything on God. Others think God is supposed to give them everything they want and if He doesn't, they write Him off.

Have you ever met anyone whose parents gave them everything they wanted? I have and it was pitiful. I never saw such a useless human being. He was in his forties and was keeping his parents broke. He didn't work, was divorced, played video games for hours, was a pervert, was a slob and regularly wasted thousands of dollars of his parent's money. I really don't believe his parents loved him at all. God is not that kind of parent.

God will not give you an easy path; He will give you a path much like Jesus' path. It will be a path with trials and tests, it will be a path with a cross, and a death but a path that will mature you and a path which like Jesus' path will end with a resurrection that leads to a throne.

Our spirit being resembles the Father's spirit being. Just as the Father has the River of Life flowing from out of His being, so Jesus told us we had Rivers of Living Water flowing from our being.

"He who believes in Me, as the scripture has said, out of his heart will flow rivers of living water." John7:38

I had a dream once, years ago. In the dream I was on our church property and there were wells all over the place. I woke up and wondered what they were. I decided to look into them in prayer even though I was awake. I found I could jump into them and start swimming down. I realized the wells were people's spirit. One belonged to my husband, there were many different people I knew. As I swam down in someone's well, I could sense who they were. But as I swam, I would usually shortly come to a barrier, and I could not swim any farther. That is until I got into Jesus well, there were no barriers in His. I could swim as deep as I wanted in His, but this time it was me that needed to turn back I could only swim so far.

Our spirits' have deep places in them, which only God knows. We have so much to learn, not just about God but about ourselves.

We are created in His image in other ways also. Just as the Bible says that God is light, *God is light and in Him is no darkness at all 1John 1:5b*the Bible also says we are light. *You are the Light of the world, Matthew 5:14*

We are to be beings of light just as our Father is. Our spirit man is created in His image. It is our light that affects the world around us. Jesus told us to let our light shine. Light chases away darkness. Darkness cannot stay where light is present. Our life can project a little tiny bit of light like a night light, or our life can be a huge beam of light. It depends on how much we allow the Lord in our lives. Think of yourself as a being of light, projecting Christ wherever you go. Oh, this light is not in the visible spectrum in our realm, but in the realm of the spirit it is very visible.

The Holy Spirit

Our soul is created in the likeness of the Holy Spirit. Katt Kerr describes how our soul is layered. It is created in layers and each layer looks like a complete whole of us.

Similarly, the Holy Spirit is a layered being. He is able to be everywhere by sending a layer of His being. A layer of His being actually comes inside of us.

These layers of our being can be in different places. The Bible tells us we are seated in heavenly places. That is because a layer of our being is in heaven. Layers of our beings can also be in places that they should not be. Satan seeks to shatter our soul and he holds layers of our soul captive and keeps them in torment. I have seen these places in prayer, but I did not understand what I was seeing until I read Anna Mendez Farrell's book about it, it was called, *Regions of Captivity.*

I have seen family members held in chains in caves during prayer. This is a layer of their soul. Even though the person there is not physically aware that they are chained there, their soul will respond to the torment. I will give you an example. I have often talked in my books about my overwhelming fear of smelling alcohol on someone's breath. This goes back to when I was a tiny child and I suffered horrible abuse from a stepfather with alcohol on his breath. Trauma will shatter your soul. All throughout my life when I have smelled alcohol on someone's breath the part of my soul held in that trauma responds. I do not respond as an adult; I respond as a small, terrified child. I wish I could tell you I have overcome this problem but so far, I haven't, but at least I understand it now.

Satan never does anything original. Whatever Satan does is a copy of the good that God does. So, the same is true about leaving a layer of our soul. There is a good side to this one too. Whenever you access something in the heavenly realm, a layer of your soul is deposited there also, and you can re-experience that heavenly realm or have the same experience again.

Remember I told you of my mountain dream. I awoke with such a marvelous feeling. I wanted to visit that dream again so I could experience that again. Well, I can go there again and again, even though I am awake, because I have left a layer of my soul in that place. I can return to that mountain and feel that wonder again. As I wrote to you about it, I revisited it. The wonder and awe returned through that layer of my soul. When we access Heaven in some way, we can always go back at will to that experience, because we have deposited a layer of our soul there only in a good way.

Our soul also deposits layers of our soul through sexual intercourse and between married people this is a good thing, but outside of marriage it is a bad thing. There are important reasons why we are not to have sex outside of marriage.

We like the Holy Spirit are created to be able to be in more than one place at the same time. We are seated in heavenly places, and we are also on earth.

Holy Spirit Laughter

I believe we are most like the Holy Spirit in the emotional realm. The Holy Spirit is the One who comes on people and causes them to laugh hysterically. This has happened to me many times, it is not uncommon. When I am praying with the Holy Spirit and that laughter comes on me, I know the answer is coming; something has broken through in the spirit realm.

One time a friend came to me and my sister Carol at church. Her husband had left her for another woman, and she was heartbroken. But she wasn't giving up on her husband. It had been going on for some time and it seemed the other woman had a greater hold on her husband, and it was hopeless. We all prayed for a bit but pretty soon I could not pray anymore. This bubble came up from inside of me and hit my throat and I started to laugh. Carol laughed too, we both laughed and laughed.

In fact, we laughed so hard we were bent over and holding our bellies. We laughed so hard tears ran out of our eyes. We laughed so hard that even though church was over, and people were just milling around the whole place turned to stare at why we were laughing so hard. In fact, every time I even tried to pray about her marriage from that time on, I would laugh. And also, if I just thought about her marriage I would giggle. We told her it was done; her husband would come back home. It took a while, but he did come home, and he has been home ever since, that was years ago.

The Holy Spirit inside us rejoiced ahead of time. He made us laugh. The Holy Spirit is full of emotion. The Holy Spirit also grieves. He grieves when things are not right and many times, I would feel that grief. I since have learned that grief is a call to stop and pray and pray and pray. The Holy Spirit has called me to pray through that grief so many times.

One time was when my oldest daughter Lonna went on a trip. She packed up her old car and set off to see a friend who lived more than a thousand miles away in Canada. She had very little money. I was not happy about the whole trip to begin with, but this was different. After she left, I was miserable. I knew it was the Holy Spirit and He was grieved, and I was grieved. I knew He was calling me to pray and that she was in danger. It lasted for several days, and I prayed continually.

Then it left, and I felt peace. I could not even try to get upset about it anymore, just peace.   Well Lonna's car broke down on her way home. She was still in Canada, and she was still over a thousand miles away. She had barely enough money for gas to get home. There she was stranded in a foreign country on the side of the road, in a more remote part of Canada. She had no cell phone service; her phone did not work there. She did not know what to do.

This could have spelled disaster and I believe she would have been in serious danger except the Holy Spirit through me had prayed this thing through. A certain man came by who was a Christian. He felt compelled to stop. He did not live there but he was traveling through to a business meeting. He picked Lonna up and had Lonna's car towed to a mechanic and paid for it to be fixed. The car needed extensive work and he took Lonna in until everything was fixed and sent her safely on her way home.

The Holy Spirit did this. It was my job to pray, but He alerted me and prayed through me and of course He altered the course of what would have happened to Lonna. Which judging by the grief I felt would not have been good.

I have heard many people say that the Holy Spirit is their best friend. Is it any wonder that we should feel that way with His constant presence that covers us, warns us, laughs and cries with us, comforts and teaches us, and even helps us to pray?

Yes, we are also created in the image of the Holy Spirit.

Jesus

Our body is created in the image of Jesus. Jesus is the part of God who physically came to earth and lived with humans. He is also a part of God that we can see and relate to. Jesse Duplantis tells in his vision of heaven about seeing that Father on His throne. The light was so bright and the power so overwhelming coming from the Father that he could not lift his head except for just a brief second and get a little peek at the Father. Then, Jesse said, that out of the light and power stepped Jesus. God in the flesh. Jesse could see Jesus.

Jesus lived among us and ate and drank with us in the flesh. He was born like us and he experienced life like we do.

But there is more, we are also the body of Christ. We are his hands and feet on earth. The same works He did on earth we can now do because we physically represent Him. Also, the body of Christ is represented as a human body. Paul said that the eye cannot say to the hand, "I have no need of you." We are represented as His body, and He is the head.

Neville Johnson has seen some amazing things in His heavenly travels. One thing he said just amazed me. He said he was taken far above heaven, and he was looking down at it from this distant place. Of course, there are many cities and places in heaven, and he also said heaven is massive. But as he looked down, he noticed it all was in the shape of a man. Of course, this was not visible from the surface of heaven only when he was taken far above it to look down on it.

Then another time he said he was taken to the very edge of the universe. As he looked at all the stars and galaxies, he noticed that the universe also was in the shape of a man.

I wonder if this has some correlation to the body of

Christ. Could some live in His hands, could some live in His heart? We have so much to learn about everything.

Jesus is also called the Word and God created the world with words. In the same way our words actually have power to change the atmosphere around us, either for good or for bad. In this way also we are like Jesus, the Creator.

Jesus now lives in a resurrected, glorified body. He can walk through walls, appear and disappear, change forms, fly, appear in many places at once, travel at the speed of thought and He will even kill the entire anti-christ army with the word of His mouth.

Jesus has a glorified human body and so will we. He will resurrect our bodies in the twinkling of an eye. Those who are in the graves, or wherever their bodies are scattered, every atom and molecule will come together, and a new resurrected body will burst forth. The dead in Christ will rise first and then those on earth will be resurrected and join them and meet the Lord in the air. Our body will soon be much like His. [1Thessalonians 4:15-18]

We like God are a tri part being. We have a spirit, soul and a body. Each of these parts have been created of the image of God our creator. There is so much more to know about God and so much more to know about ourselves. But for a start let's just realize, He made us. We are special to Him and He loves us. We are fearfully and wonderfully made. We can continue on in God and become yet even more in His image. We still yet have so much to learn about who we are, and the great things God has put inside of us. Things from Himself because we are created in His image.

Chapter Fourteen

IMAGINATION

Our imagination is another way we are created in Gods image. It is a very important part of you. It is a screen with which we view the unseen. It is very real and given to you by God. It is powerful. Of course, Satan wants to pervert this screen and fill your imagination with evil things, such as pornography. This is to block you from the godly use of your imagination. Jesus said in the Sermon on the Mount that the pure in heart would see God. Those with a pure heart have not muddied up the screen of their imagination, or the eyes of their heart. Many times, children are way ahead of us in imagination because their hearts are so pure.

A Child's Imagination

One of my favorite days of my whole life happened

about five years ago. It was a late August day and I unexpectedly got out of work early. The day was hot and very windy with a stiff breeze out of the south. I knew the waves on my favorite beach would be the big kind that I love to jump and swim in, and I wanted to go!

I decided to go pick up my two grandsons, David, five years old, and Franky, four, to go with me. They love to swim as much as I do. I saw to that by bringing them swimming as much as I could. I was correct they wanted to come but their mother told me as I picked them up that David's kindergarten orientation was that night at 6:30, and I had to have the boys to the school by then. We had several hours so we headed to the lake.

As soon as I parked the car both boys jumped out and headed for the water. David stopped threw up his little hands and cried, "Oh the wind, the waves, the sun, it's a beautiful day!!!"

David had given his heart to the Lord at age four and he sees God in nature and creation, it all makes God real to him.

The three of us ran and jumped into the waves squealing with delight. It was so fun I felt I could stay forever. But after about forty-five minutes David swam off from Franky and I and then went to shore. We watched him wondering what in the world he was doing and what could be more fun than swimming. He was busily walking to and fro and doing things. Finally, I called to him, "David what are you doing? Don't you want to swim?"

"I can't," David responded, "I found a dog."

"What dog?"

"He's invisible."

So that's what he was doing, he was playing with a dog.

He was running with it and petting it and playing games. He was totally captivated by the dog and played with it the rest of the afternoon while Franky and I swam without him.

In the car on the way home David held his dog on his lap petting him lovingly.

"What should I name him?' he asked me.

I could not believe something invisible was so real to him and that he was so attached to this invisible dog, I was rather amazed.

"Well, Rover is a good dog's name," I said.

"Rover, that's it his name is Rover!" David cried.

Franky, not to be outdone by his brother declared that he had three cats sitting on his lap.

We headed home and got ready for the kindergarten orientation, the boys continuing to hold and play with their new pets. Soon it was time to go. The elementary school is just behind my house across a field, so we walked over. David put Rover on a leash, {Invisible leash} and was holding it as we crossed the field. Franky said his cats were following us. We went into the school and found David's classroom.

David is very outgoing, but Franky has a tendency to be very shy. As soon as we got in the school Franky forgot about his cats and grabbed my leg so tight, I could hardly walk.   But David marched in his new classroom holding Rover's leash and marched up to his new teacher and announced, "Hi, I'm David."

I was stuck at the door because Franky was clutching my leg so hard, I couldn't move, and he was hiding behind me the best he could.

David's teacher noticed David holding the leash and said to him, "Is that your dog?"

"Yes," David responded and then motioning over toward me and Franky who was barely visible hiding behind me, he added, "And that's my brother Franky over there, he's the one with all the cats!"

That has been five years ago, and I am still laughing!

It amazed me that what David was seeing with his imagination was so real to him. It was so real, even though he was having an amazing fun time swimming he stopped when he found the dog. Then he played with the dog for the rest of the afternoon. And later he even introduced Franky as the one with all the cats! His little eyes were seeing something the rest of us did not see.

Jesus said, "Blessed are the pure in heart for they shall see God."

Our imaginations are a very real gift from God. They are very important. In this way we also have been created in God's image. Like God we have an imagination. We can be creators just as He is. He has given us the screen to see the unseen and to God the unseen is real. It is so real that we are responsible for what we allow to project on this invisible screen.

"You have heard it said to those of old, 'You shall not commit adultery.' But I say to you that whosoever looks at a woman to lust for her has already committed adultery with her in his heart."   Matthew 5:27-28

Imaginary Sin is Real Sin

We are actually held accountable for an imaginary adultery, because this thing called the imagination is something real in the spirit realm. I have heard it taught that the imagination is the bridge to the spirit realm. Our imagination gives us the ability to create and change things in the natural realm and what we allow on this screen is very important.

I have also heard it taught that Satan does not have this ability. He cannot create. He only copies what God has and perverts it. He has nothing original. Everything he does is a perversion of something real and good. He wants to destroy, and pervert mankind's use of their imaginations and he does this by vile images.

Some examples of this would be pornography, video games, violence or horror on television or movies. These things have absolutely no place in the life of a believer. We are to keep our imaginations pure if we are to see God and peer into the spirit realm. We do this with our imaginations. We look with the eyes of our hearts.

Lessons in my Imagination

When I first became a Christian, I would use my imagination as I would ride the bus to school. We lived out of town and had a long ride to school. The sun would just be coming up and the scenery was beautiful. I would picture myself worshipping the Lord in the misty fields we passed. Soon my imagination would stop, and a vision would start. It was no longer me imagining but me watching.

I will tell you about one of them. I was fourteen when I got saved and I had spent my whole life wishing I was someone else. I always felt ugly, shy and unpopular. I hated my frizzy hair and the fact that I had to wear glasses. It had never even occurred to me to like myself and who I was. I always wanted to be someone else.

One day as I was worshipping the Lord in the fields, in my imagination. I decided to put some of the girls from school that needed to know the Lord in the field with us. Kind of like a prayer. I picked the popular girls at school. [not that I knew them, I was a dud, but I wanted them to know the Lord.] I put them in the vision with me and we were all dancing around Jesus in the beautiful morning mist.

As we were dancing and I looked around the circle, I felt horrified. They were so much prettier than me. One girl had long gorgeous hair past her waist. My hair was awful compared to hers. I thought the Lord would never look at me again because the other girls had hair that was so much prettier than I did. Suddenly as I watched all of our hair disappeared. None of us had hair. We looked funny, but I liked it, because I wanted the Lord to love me as much as them.

The scene continued. I would look around the circle at their pretty faces and it would happen again. I would think, "They are so much prettier than me. The Lord will never look at me." Then suddenly all our faces disappeared. The same with our clothes, suddenly we were all dressed in white. Finally, we all looked rather plain, but the same, and I was content that I was not the ugly duckling in the crowd. The rest of the morning we all worshipped the Lord on my way to school.

The Lord was teaching me something I had no concept of at that age. That my worth to Him was not in my appearance. That I was no less to Him than all these girls whose lives I had idolized and wished I could be. He taught me with pictures on the screen of my imagination.

Seeing Angels

It was many, many years later before I ever heard any teaching on imagination but still very little. I had ordered a Christian book online and it came with a teaching tape. The tape was about seeing angels. The lady on the tape said to ask God where the angel is standing in the room. When you get an impression then look with your spiritual eyes or your imagination until you get some sort of image, maybe a color or something and keep focusing until you see it.

I tried it and I could get a vague outline of angels. I shared the tape with my daughter, Joy, and suddenly she could see angels clearly and even talk to them. I was kind of jealous I wanted to see what she was seeing.

"Just look," she told me one day as we were praying together. I was peering in, but I could only dimly make out the image of an angel. It was like my sight without my glasses, very blurry, I am terribly near-sighted.

Suddenly the angel I was looking at put his face right up to my face and I could see him clearly, we were face to face! He had the most delightful smile. I knew he must be Joy's angel because his facial features were almost identical to hers. I gasped with excitement. I did not know angels had such a sense of humor.

One of my very favorite teachers, Neville Johnson, has a free online school. He understands about imagination. He teaches that our imagination is real and what we see in it is very real. That is because of our ability to create. Neville has had amazing experiences that totally captivate me. He has seen heaven talked with the Lord, angels and past saints and has even seen into the millennium. I love to hear him teach. He emphasizes the importance of the imagination.

Not only is our imagination an important part of us created by God, but it is also another way that we are created like God. God used His imagination to create us. We were created with an inner screen. We can project on this screen and so can God. This screen is an important part of our spiritual anatomy, it is another set of eyes so to speak, the eyes of our heart.

It is very important to keep a pure screen, don't watch any foul stuff. The Bible says the pure in heart will see God. This inner screen has something to do with us being creators like God. God has an imagination, and we are a product of it.

We have existed inside of God for eons, in a real place, a very real place; we lived and played in that place. We existed inside of God's imagination.

Chapter Fifteen

CREATED TO LOVE

You shall love the Lord your God with all your heart, soul mind and strength and you shall love your neighbor as yourself. Luke 10:27

We are created in God's image, so we are created to love. Whether we pass this test of life or not depends on whether we learn to love or not. There are many forces in this universe, but the greatest is love. Our eternal position will depend on whether we learn to love or not. Our level of love will be our level, our position, our level of success and our level of joy.

We live in a world filled with hate; how can we love? We have been taught and trained the opposite of love our whole lives and even what we think of love is often selfishness.

When I was a new wife, I prayed constantly for my husband to change. He was wild and out of control. One day while I was praying God interrupted my prayers and told me that I was not praying out of love for my husband, I was praying for God to change my husband because I wanted my life to be easier. I was not praying a prayer God could answer. I was praying selfishly, and I wanted God to serve me by making my life easier. I had a lot of changing to do. God had a bigger project than making my life easier; He was teaching me to love my husband unconditionally. That was much more important than my life being easy.

Being created in His image means we have to put off the old man and start putting on the new one. It means that our reaction to others must be God's reaction and that is to love, even your enemies.

Our level of love, our level of how much we become like Christ, is the level of authority that we will be trusted with in our eternal position. I can see how important it was that God did not answer my selfish prayer and make my life easier. And my life did not become any easier for many years. {You can read about that in my book *The Impossible Marriage*.} My prayers did not get answered until I learned to love my husband unconditionally.

God was forming the image of His Son in me, but yet it was not all about me. It was all about His kingdom come and His will being done in my life, in my husband's life, in my family and in what we can bring to the Body of Christ. It had to stop being about me.

I had to learn to follow only God's voice. His voice led me to love. His voice led me to life, through the tumultuous years of living through my husband's alcoholism. God brought heaven to me in the midst of our hell. {Believe me it was hell; my husband was a mean drunk} He did it through love. I could never have done it on my own. I had to constantly bring Him

118

the rage, the fear, the confusion, the pain, and follow His plan, to love and forgive, to love and forgive and to love and forgive.

There were so many voices that told me to do the opposite of what God was telling me. Voices of people that meant well but they were not God's voice. They thought I should divorce Jim because it was tough. If I had followed their voices instead of God's I would not have learned to love.

Many different pastors told me throughout the years that I had married out of God's will. I would argue with them that, "No, I did not marry out of God's will." But it was to no avail. I never convinced one of them. And then they would say, {How could so many different people say exactly the same thing, but they did}, then they would all say, "Well you will just have to make the best of it." In other words, endure for the rest of your life, with this hopeless situation, because you blew it.

But God was in charge and my marriage was His will. It was never about enduring but about all of us becoming like Christ through it and learning to love, all of us, my husband, myself and my three children.

And that is what our lives on this earth are about, yours and mine and everybody's. It is about being transformed into the image of Christ, by following Him and learning to live and love like Him. Turning to Him again and again as life gives us impossible situations and learning and receiving the ability to handle each situation in His strength and in His power, the power of love.

Please forgive me if you think I am making it sound easy because it is not easy. It was not easy, and it is still not easy. Something inside of us always seems to want revenge, to want what is fair or to want justice. Oh, I have tried all those things too. I have fought with my husband. I have poured out bottles and bottles of alcohol. I have tried to hurt my husband. I have even run him over with the car and I have spent time in jail for domestic violence. Take it from me, don't do it that way.

The wrath of man does not produce the righteousness of God. James 1:20

We forget the cross! We take up our cross and follow Jesus. It is the only way.

The bottom line is love and being formed into the image of Christ. We can emanate love, {Christ}. If we emanate love, we carry heaven to earth. We can create an atmosphere of heaven around us, in our homes, in our families, or wherever we go.

The original plan for this earth was for Adam to make earth like heaven. Instead, Adam fell, and Satan took his place, and the earth was filled with darkness and sin. But now through Christ we can begin to take back our rightful authority by living the same way He did and allowing Him to live through you, LOVE.

I did not realize it, but it is all there in the Bible. Read the red words, the ones Jesus spoke. He said we should never repay evil for evil. He said we should turn the other cheek. He said we should overcome evil with good. He said we should forgive 70 times 7. He not only said it, but He also lived it.

He was showing us how to do it, how to live, how to retake dominion, in our lives, in our families, in our homes and wherever we go. Our level of love is our level of authority but not just for now, for all of eternity!

God is love; it is the nature of His being. You were created in His image; you were created to love. Love is the most powerful force in the universe. Love has a color and a smell and a light it carries. It is a force and a power. It overcomes evil and it never ever, ever fails. The opposite of love is not hate; the opposite of love is pride and selfishness which causes fear. The opposite of love is it being all about me.

That is where I was, it was all about me. God used a hard situation, my marriage, to save me from selfishness and from fear and to form the image of His Son in me. I wanted things to change and in a hurry! Nothing changed until I changed, until I learned to love.

Chapter Sixteen

LOST IDENTITY

Our identity is how we see ourselves. It is a big deal. Some may see themselves as a ballerina and that becomes their identity. Someone else may see themselves as an athlete and that becomes their identity. This gives a person a goal to work toward and helps them develop a talent. But what happens if they have an injury, and that door becomes closed.

What happens to their identity?

I recently heard a man tell of how his whole life was sports and that was his identity. When he was hurt and had to stop playing, he was devastated and began to run with the wrong crowd and ended up on drugs. His identity was lost.

Others may get their identity from how their family or parents see them. This is the smart kid, or this is our pretty one, or this is the bad kid.

Seeing yourself as the smart one is not all bad because it may spur you on to get an education and keep you out of a life of drugs. On the other hand, being the pretty one is a very short-lived identity, beauty quickly fades and if that is where your self-worth came from what happens if you find your looks gone? Do you see yourself as worthless?

And then there are the foolish parents who label a kid as bad. You have damaged his self-worth and he will live up to being bad.

My identity is something I have struggled with my whole life. I struggled with it as a young person and then again in my forties. Because of a traumatic childhood I lost who I was. The person in me was swallowed up by fear and never developed. I felt like a non-person. I did not learn to overcome this overnight it took many years, and I am still learning it.

One of the first things I rejected was my appearance. God had to teach me my value isn't in my appearance. No one's is. Even a very beautiful person cannot hang onto their beauty, it fades. To accept or reject yourself or others based on appearance is totally contrary to God and His ways.

There are some people through disease or malformations who are hideously ugly. This does not lessen their value at all. It also does not lesson their beauty to God. They may in fact be more beautiful depending on how they develop their spirit. If we are to become like God, we cannot continue to value ourselves or others on appearance.

The reason this lesson is so hard to learn is we live in a world that worships beauty. In your teenage years this lesson is almost impossible to fathom. The pretty girls get asked on dates, get parts in plays, or become prom queens. The rest of us can be invisible, or so it seems. The real truth is that absolutely no one is invisible to God. Their importance is astounding.

No Such Thing as Nobodies

We got a little glimpse of this at our prayer meeting one day. My sister Carol, my daughter Joy and I meet weekly to pray. This particular day we were praying, and we prayed for someone who was famous who had been in the news, I can't even remember who it was now or what their problem was. But after we prayed, I thought to myself, "We prayed for this person because they were famous and we knew about them, but there are a lot of nobody's with the same problem, but no one knows because they are not famous."

So, I began to pray for the nobodies with the same problem, because only God knew who they were.

Immediately God spoke prophetically through Joy. He said, "There are no such things as nobodies to Me. Every single person is a celebrity to Me, each person is famous and precious to Me."

I gasped, but it's true. God has each of us on a stage so to speak. We are His stars. He loves us and watches us with delight. It is His desire that we turn to Him and dwell with Him forever. He even assigns teams of angels to stay with us and guard us. We are all His superstars, and He has a special and unique plan for each one of us and it is just not for the few little years we are on earth. It stretches forward through eons of time, and it is beyond your wildest dreams.

God is in Us

I recently read a book by a man named Jim Woodward. I loved it. This man was clinically brain dead for eleven hours and during that time he had quite an experience. Jim had not lived at all for the Lord, he had lived for himself. In his last seconds of life, he asked God to forgive him.

Jim found himself in a place between heaven and hell. As he was standing over a pit that led to hell a gate opened and the most horrible demonic creature came toward him to bring him to hell. He was horrified that this horrid creature called him by name. Just as Jim thought he was done for he cried out to God for help. Immediately three huge angels appeared and rescued him. They were huge and beautiful; one stood about fifteen feet tall. Jim was awestruck; they were so majestic.

But then something amazing happened. Something that struck me when I read it and the reason, I am writing this to you. Although Jim felt wretched because in this state, he realized he had led a selfish life and he felt unworthy before these majestic angels, all three angels bowed to him! Amazed Jim asked them why and he was told it was because the light of God was within him.

We are amazing creatures with unbelievable value, and it has nothing at all to do with our appearance. It has to do with being created in God's image and it has to do with the fact that he has put Himself inside of us!!!

I Felt Worthless because I was Poor

Even though God started immediately dealing with me

about my identity in Him when I got saved, I had a long way to go. In my twenties I rejected myself again. This time because of poverty. Early in our marriage my husband, Jim and I just could not make it financially. I felt so worthless. I wrote a story for a magazine about this time in my life. I am going to include part of it here because it captures how worthless I felt.

One winter day, my sister Carol was driving me around town. I couldn't afford insurance on my own car. I was trying to bring a clock back to a factory outlet where I had purchased it a year before. It had never worked, but I had never gotten around to bringing it back. Now I was pregnant and broke. I wanted some groceries. I was hoping to get the twenty dollars back I had paid for it.

It didn't work. I looked so shabby. I didn't have a winter coat that fit me. I was wearing one of my husband's sweat jackets and a vest over the top of that. I felt so worthless. Trying to scrounge up some money and looking like a fool made me feel worse. The lady hadn't believed me and wouldn't give me a refund. I sat in my sister's car and cried, mostly out of humiliation.

In retrospect, I see my self-worth was tied to my net worth. At this point in my life both were at zero. On the way back home my sister and I stopped off at my dad's house. He had called and said he had a bag for me on his porch. He hadn't said what was in the bag, just that he had a bag for me.

Carol waited in the car for me as I ran on the porch. I saw a paper bag full of groceries with a T-bone steak sticking out of the top. I was about to pick it up when I saw another plastic bag full of dirt [actually it was potting soil.]

I froze.

"What if I am supposed to take the dirt?"

I stood there frozen between the dirt and the groceries. I must have stood there for some time because Carol came stomping in to see what was taking me so long.

"What's the matter," she huffed, "Let's go!"

"I don't know what bag I am supposed to take the groceries or the potting soil."

"The groceries," she said swooping them up. "Why would dad give you a bag of dirt?"

Because of the poverty my husband and I were going through I felt that we were totally worthless. I saw a bag of dirt and I felt like that was all I deserved.

I had been so trained in my life that money was important and that being poor made me feel utterly worthless. The Lord had to retrain me some more, and He did. It all came to a head one day at church during a communion service. I felt so low during this period in my life that whenever I went to church, the tears would start and there was nothing I could do to stop them.

This day was no different. It was time for communion, and we were all holding our little crackers and our little plastic cups of grape juice.

As usual a steady stream of tears was flowing down my face. I did not even feel worthy to sit with these people. They were together and I was nothing but a mess. We were supposed to be preparing our hearts for communion, but I couldn't, I was too broken. Instead, I decided to just picture Jesus on the cross. The pain in my heart was so great that it was easy to picture pain and agony. I could clearly see Jesus suffering before me on the cross.

As I watched Him, we silently suffered together. Then I

noticed a large drop of blood forming on His brow, as I was watching it suddenly dropped from His face and plopped in my cup I was holding. It was so real that it surprised me and with a little start I opened my eyes. I gasped in wonder and amazement. A drop of Jesus' blood had actually fallen in my cup. I was holding a drop of His blood.

Then suddenly as I looked around the room, everyone's little plastic cups of grape juice stood out to me. I saw a sea of little plastic cups, each holding a single drop of Jesus blood. The exact same portion as I had.

We were equal. We all had the same portion, one drop of blood. All of a sudden, I had worth. I had the same portion of worth as each person. My worth was that drop of blood. My tears stopped as I sat in awe of my newfound worth.

Our worth has absolutely nothing at all to do with our financial status. The poorest man on earth has the exact same value as the richest. Worldly wealth is absolutely nothing in value compared to a single drop of the blood of Jesus, which has an unbelievable, inconceivable weight of value on an eternal scale. Those without this treasure suffer incredible loss for all eternity but those who have it will live like kings forever.

I had many more bouts with my identity but the biggest one was yet to come, my mid-life crisis. In a spiritual battle Satan stole my identity.

Chapter Seventeen

SATAN SEEKS TO CAPTURE OUR IDENTITY

It is Satan's plan and purpose to steal your identity. He wants to steal your identity so he can steal your destiny which God has created for you. This is an unfathomable loss of eternal proportions. In fact, Satan has launched his greatest attack ever on this generation. He has unleashed many weapons, one such being his attack on the sexuality of this generation.

A friend I knew from high school's grown son has changed himself to a girl. Satan has launched an attack on his identity. Never has a generation had such an attack on their identity. He has declared war on this generation because he fears this generation more than any other generation. Why?

This generation has been called to retake what he has stolen. We have great purpose. This is the generation that will find out who we really are in Christ and stand up to Satan. This is the generation that will come to our full stature in Christ. It is fearful to Satan, but it is glorious to us. And even all of nature has been groaning and longing for this day!

Satan wants to steal your destiny by stealing your identity. It happened to me in my forties, and it was horrible. I rejected myself again. I did not even see it coming. Although God gave me a warning, I blew it off, I didn't think I was vulnerable. He told me, "You are the same age your mother was when she got into trouble in her marriage."

"I love Jim," I told the Lord, "I don't even look at other men, or have anything to do with them."

But in one day Satan robbed me of my identity and it took years to recover. It had nothing to do with me at first but with my teenage daughter. An older man had fallen in love with her, and I was furious about it. This man worked with her, and he was a general manager with a good job. She came to me for help because she didn't know how to handle it, so we decided she would quit her job and go stay with her brother for a while.

She still had to work one last day and I thought this man would not dare try to see her because he had been reprimanded. But just to be sure I decided to go with her for her last day at work. I wish now we would have just had her not go because I got caught that night in a spiritual trap.

I hadn't realized how attracted she was to him, even though she wanted out of the situation, and I didn't realize how attracted he was to her. He tried everything he could that night to get alone with her. Every time I get into trouble it usually through compassion, I actually felt sorry for him and left them alone. It was a spiritual battle and I lost.

Joy left the next day, and she got out of the situation, but I did not. Something terrible had happened to me. The first thing I noticed was that my mind became confused, and I couldn't think. I also stopped sleeping for more than an hour or so at night. My thinking changed.

I had been happy with everything in my life, my marriage, I loved serving the Lord, I loved being a grandma, I loved church. I was happy being me, I knew I was older and overweight but that really didn't concern me at all. I was content.

Suddenly my life seemed awful, we had always been poor and for quite a few years I had to become the provider in the family. My thinking changed about this man, I thought if Joy was with someone who made a lot of money, she would never end up like me. Somehow, I totally rejected myself. I was poor, fat, ugly and old and I had to work all the time. It was not intentional, I tried to pray off these awful feelings. I prayed in tongues for eight hours straight, all night long, I wasn't sleeping, I had time.

My emotions totally did not belong to me anymore. Nothing in my life interested me anymore. I wanted to be young, I was filled with lustful thoughts, and I was bored!

This was not me at all. It was so overpowering that I could not even think normal. Summer no longer existed, my identity was gone, and my emotions did not belong to me at all. I was obsessed with terrible thoughts. My walk with the Lord seemed gone. I actually grounded myself to the house and did not go anywhere because I knew I would get into trouble. I was so bored I longed for excitement. My kids' lives seemed so exciting, I wanted to be them.

To tell you an example of how different I was, the only kind of music I liked was worship music. I could no longer listen to worship music, I wanted to hear loud fast music. I was dressing different. I was doing everything differently.

I wondered if anyone anywhere ever went through anything like this ever. It lasted for months, and I just kept praying. I wondered if this is what happens to people who run off with someone else. During this time my husband seemed very boring. My husband has been so hurt in his life that I told the Lord I would rather die than ever hurt him, and I purposed to get me back.

It was about four months when I remember thinking I had actually felt content for about an hour, which was a breakthrough. But it took several years before I actually felt normal. I really hate writing about this. I would rather just forget it. But if someone else has had their identity stolen, I want them to know you can get you back. You can love yourself again, your own life again and love your mate again and feel content again.

During that time the Lord spoke to me, I didn't even know how I felt but He summed it up for me. He knew exactly what I was going through. He said,

"I hear your heart, it is calling to Me day and night,
it says, 'What about me? What about me?'
I've heard you.
You've waited.
You've done as best as you could, and you've trusted.
And you've seen My abundance bless those around you. And

you think life has passed you by and you are a bridge between heaven and hell and others cross over on you, but you are not allowed to enter. And you have paid a price for others.

I am bringing you into My garden.

You have rejected yourself, but I haven't rejected you.

You see a life lost and wasted, but there are desires you have that need to be laid down. Lay them at my feet, give them to Me."

Slowly I got back the things I lost. One thing that really helped me accept myself even though the trial had passed was writing my first book, *The Impossible Marriage*. I realized my life was my life and I wouldn't have it any other way.

Satan is stealing many people's identity; he does this through a broken image of ourselves. He gets us to reject ourselves and he takes us captive. This is why there is so many problems with homosexuality and trans gender problems in this day and age. Satan is seeking to steal the destinies of a generation.

In this time of my life Satan had convinced me of some lies I had to lay down at the feet of Jesus, some of them were,

That I needed to be important,

That I needed to be noticed,

That I needed to be beautiful,

That I needed to have fun all the time.

Actually, all those things were not me at all. But somehow, I had swallowed them.

I read a horrible story in the paper about a man, a supposed Christian. He actually killed his wife and two sons because he had an affair with a woman and wanted to run off with her and not have it cost him anything. Do you think Satan stole his destiny?

Yes, he hijacked his emotions to the point he was so cold to own wife and children that he killed his own family. How sickening. He rejected his life and his destiny. This is serious stuff.

We have to accept ourselves, our life, our mate. We have to lay down every emotion and desire at His feet. Our own life and destiny are just too wonderful to miss. I have to tell you; I am so glad to have me back!

Chapter Eighteen

BRAINWASHED BY THE WORLD

From the time we are born we begin to be brainwashed into thinking the opposite of the truth. The spirit of this world, the prince of the power of the air seeks to form us into the image of Satan and not of God. When we come to God, His ways are totally foreign to us. I have come to realize that we {And I am including myself} just Christianize the same old junk that the world does. Very few of us actually live like Jesus taught us to. We read it, we agree with it, but we don't do it.

What do I mean by that? We still are trying to live for ourselves we just think God is supposed to help achieve that end. We try to use faith to get what we want. Is that what faith is for, to get what we want? Most of the time, what we want is money, or stuff? And it probably will work, God set us up that way, we can believe and receive. Faith works as much for the unbeliever as the believer. And there are many Christians believing for the things they want.

But is that what we are supposed to be using faith for?

In the end will God be pleased with your life if that is what you used your faith for?

I think of Stephen in the Bible, he was called a man of great faith. He used to his faith not to get rich, but to lay down his life for the gospel. To stand firm and not to waver. He bravely held his testimony to the end and prayed for his persecutors as he was dying. Now that is what I call faith!

There are big time preachers on television that teach to use faith for money, and they are so rich. Some of them are worth 25-50 million dollars. And they are constantly asking for more money! Why don't they use their own?

Jesus taught us something in the Sermon on the Mount. He said, "Why do you worry, saying, 'What do we eat?' or 'What do we drink?' or, 'What shall we wear?' For the pagans run after all these things. But seek first the kingdom of God and all these things will be given to you."

So, Jesus told us it's the world that run after things, but God wants us to seek His kingdom, and He will give us what we need. We are not really getting it though, we are still running after the things, not the kingdom, just like the pagans.

I still don't get it, at all, how so many preachers preach all this rich stuff because I am not rich at all and in my own life God has dealt with me about having too many things. I'm not really against being rich, believe me, I would love to be rich. I am against it being our focus.

We Christianize other things from the world also. What we want just looks different now. We want to be a big cheese in the church world and have our name be known. We want to be known in the church as the super spiritual one. If that is you, you are in good company. The disciples of Jesus got in a big fight about which one of them would be the greatest in the kingdom of heaven. Then two of them sent their mother after Jesus trying to get on the two thrones next Jesus in heaven. This is when Jesus sat them down and taught them about humility and being a servant. Jesus told them in the world, the big shots lord it over others but in His kingdom to be great you must be a servant. He also said we need to become as a little child.

And there is more, we still gossip and backbite it just comes in the form of a prayer request. "Pray for sister Sue, I saw her in the grocery store with booze in her cart."

There is a whole new way to live, and we are not getting it.

I remember back in the days when God wanted me to go to AL anon. Al anon is a group that goes along with AA {Alcoholics Anonymous} Only AL anon is for the wife or husband of the drinker. I would not go. I tell about it in my book, *The Impossible Marriage.* I did not want to waste my time. I wanted to be in church meetings and prayer meetings, not a non-Christian meeting. Besides, I did not need it, or so I thought. God actually had to get me arrested sent to jail and ordered by the court to go to Al anon. {Yes, I can be stubborn.}

So, I had to go to Al anon. But something amazed me. They actually had a better take on God than the church. I learned something powerful in AL anon. It was in the twelve steps. Actually, there is a lot of good stuff in the twelve steps, but it was the eleventh step that astounded me.

Step 11 Sought through prayer and meditation to improve our conscious contact with God, as we understood Him, praying only for the knowledge of His will and the power to carry that out.

What! I could not believe what I was reading! Praying **only** for the knowledge of His will and the power to carry that out! I absolutely could not BELIEVE WHAT I WAS READING!!!!!

I had been a Christian for many years. Not just a Christian, my whole purpose in life was to be a Christian. I thought I knew it all! I spent my life trying to know it all about being a Christian. I read through the Bible over and over. I read almost every book in our church library. When I couldn't afford the new ones, I would go in the Bible bookstore and pick up a book and quick read a chapter, set it down, and come in another day and quick read another. I mean I thought I knew it all!

Praying only for the knowledge of His will and the ability to carry it out!!!!!!!!!!!!!!!!!!

What!!!!!!!!!!!!!!!!!!!!!!!!!!!!!!

I had been doing it backwards all these years. I had been praying for Him to know what I wanted and trying so hard to get Him to carry it out!

I am supposed to be praying to know what He wants and me carry it out.

I am shocked. No wonder I was having so much trouble getting God to do what I wanted to do. I am praying and praying all these years for God to do what I want.

{Hey, I read hundreds of books on name it and claim it and all the ways to manipulate God with faith.}

I realized that the church was missing it too. I was a product of the church. God had to send me to a secular meeting to straighten me out.

Just because we are Christians does not mean we are not brainwashed by the world. There is a whole new way of thinking and it's all there in the Bible and especially in the gospels, but I was just not getting it.

Do It

The Sermon on the Mount tells us how to live. The problem is we read it, but we don't do it.

It reminds me of my husband when he went to AA. Jim had been in and out of treatment centers for alcohol and drug addiction since before we were married. Since we were married, he's been in even more. All of them use the twelve steps. He had been in hundreds of AA meetings. Every meeting begins with reading the twelve steps. Jim had probably read the twelve steps hundreds of times. But Jim did not get it. We can read something over and over and just not get it.

I heard someone ask Jim after many years, "Have you done the twelve steps?"

Jim looked confused and said, "Done the twelve steps? The twelve steps aren't something you do, there something you read."

That day talking to that man, Jim finally realized after reading the twelve steps all those years, the Twelve Steps were more than just something you read to open the meeting, they are something you actually do!

I thought that was so funny, I really had a good laugh. But I was just like him, only it was the Bible I had been reading for years.

We are all like Jim. We have read the Sermon on the Mount for years; most people can recite many parts of it. I had actually memorized the whole thing; I had read it and read it for years like Jim had the twelve steps. All of a sudden, I realized, it is something we are actually supposed to be doing! Not just reading!!!

How many people have we seen get sued and they gave someone more than they were suing them for? I would have to say never. But it's in the Sermon on the Mount. There is a lot of tough stuff in that sermon.

Recently a Christian woman who was my age was ogling some good-looking guy. This is what she said, "Well, I can look can't I?"

Well, no, you can't, not according to the Sermon on the Mount. In fact, according to that she had just committed adultery. We have been brainwashed by the world to think, and act opposite to the ways of God. The answer is in our hands, but we have got to do more than read it. We have to do it.

Brain washed by Movies and Television

The plot of every movie and play, and television show is almost always teaching us the wrong messages. Some of the main ones are revenge, follow your own heart and at all costs be happy, do your own thing, and you can be happy without God.

Who do you think is behind these messages? It sounds like the devil to me. Somehow Satan managed to deceive one third of the angels into believing this stuff and they fell. Now he is on the earth propagating his lies to humans, and they live by it, and look at the condition of the world.

Can you imagine Chuck Norris or Rambo, turning the other cheek, or overcoming their enemy with love? No, the whole idea of action movies is to whip men into a frenzy of revenge and then rejoicing as the object of their anger is pummeled with karate chops or bullets from machine guns.

But let's not be too hard on the men, the romance movies idolize romance like it is the answer to life. A perfect, handsome, often rich, stranger appears who has absolutely no flaws and puts our starlet on a pedestal. He is so perfect and all he has to do in life is passionately pursue her.

We are so full of stars in our eyes as we turn off the television longing for the passion we have seen displayed, that we rush to our own husbands hoping for the same twinkle, only to find him sprawled out on the bed eating ice cream and watching his own show in his old grungy jeans and his socks that smell so bad we run reeling for the air freshener. And if we are so impassioned, we get past the stinky socks he says, "Not now honey I am watching the baseball game."

Suddenly we are discontented with our life.

Oh, and let's talk about the show I can't stand the most, MASH. We have the slovenly, lustful, constantly drinking martinis, doctor who disrespects authority as our hero. Somehow as the wounded come in, he suddenly sobers up and performs perfectly in the operating room. He never marries because he is constantly chasing women and yet the married man in the story who respects authority is painted as a moron. What is that show teaching?

We have to stop agreeing with the world! I was complaining the other day to a friend about a young preteen boy I saw on Facebook who had a repost filled with profanity and lauding everyone's choice of freedom meaning homosexuality. I was upset because the boy's own supposedly Christian mother had pressed *like* to the filthy post and given it her approval. The women I was talking to, also a Christian, responded that young children need to learn about homosexuals.

Uh..what? We need to teach our children the mindset of the world. **No,** all they need to know is what the Bible says about homosexuality, and that only, because the Bible is truth. They don't need this other stuff!

Guess what? The young people today are being brainwashed by the world, {Satan]. Guess what? It is not just the kids.

We have to shut out the voices of the world, {Satan], and replace it with the Bible, {God}. That means quit watching television and movies, reading the latest novel and um entertaining yourself with the things of the world, {Satan}. If you must have entertainment there is the PureFlix channel or the Dove channel.

But seriously, we have work to do. We need to get unbrainwashed by the truth. It's called renewing your mind and it's done by replacing these lies with the truth in the word. Let's start with the Sermon on the Mount, and then move on to all the other words written in red, Jesus's words. And remember it is not just something you read it is something that you do.

Do you remember how the Sermon on the Mount ends? I will write it for you because it is a great way to end this chapter.

*"Therefore, whoever hears these sayings of Mine, and **does** them, I will liken him to a wise man who built his house on the rock; and the rain descended, the floods came, and the winds blew and beat on that house; and it did not fall, for it was founded on the rock.*

"But everyone who hears these sayings of Mine and

does not do them, will be like a foolish man who built his house on the sand; and the rain descended, the floods came, and the winds blew and beat on that house; and it fell. And great was its fall" Matthew7;24-27

Chapter Nineteen
A NEW IDENTITY

I have been crucified with Christ; it is no longer I who live but Christ lives in me and the life which I now live in the flesh, I live by faith in the Son of God, who loved me and gave Himself for me. Galatians 2:20

When we become born again, we begin a new life with a new identity. I used to wonder if that meant that we gave up our personality and gave up who we are. That kind of rubbed me wrong, not that I had much of a personality, but it seemed strange, to stop being who we are, and be Christ instead. I wanted to still be Summer, something in this scripture bothered me. Do we give up who we are and just all become Jesus'?

I now realize actually just the opposite is true. Jesus is the One who gave up who He was. He was the Word, the eternal Word, one with God in heaven. He had to become a human, the Son of Man to restore our broken identity.

We were created in God's image, originally, but we had begun to look more like Satan. He is prideful, self-centered, and self-serving. This is what fallen man has become. Our original identity has been shattered. We were not created for sin, lust, pride greed, jealousy, selfishness, perversion, idolatry, etc...

Jesus is the One who has given up who He was so He could become what we were created to be. Now through Him, what we were created to be has been restored. We were created to love, to have peace, to worship God and have fellowship with Him. What dies is the fallen man we had become. That is what ceases to exist. GOOD RIDDANCE!

This is what baptism is about. Baptism is a powerful thing. We can't forget about baptism. It was powerful for me. I had actually gotten saved the week before I was baptized. I had lived like the devil before I was saved. Then when I did get saved, I tried to tell everyone I knew what had happened to me, but it was like I was speaking another language. They did not know what I was talking about. The day after I gave my heart to God, I went out to find the old gang of friends and I found them. I had some pot stashed and they had found it and they were all smoking it. My first reaction was anger, but then I realized I was over that, I was living for God now.

"I've got God now," I said to blank stares. They didn't get it. I went home disappointed. But when they heard I was going to be baptized, that seemed to sink in.

I realize now God had my baptism all planned. Our church baptistery was broken so I was very publicly baptized in the lake we lived on, in our front yard, for all the neighbors and friends who saw me live like the devil to see. The whole church followed us home after the service; like a parade, parked all over the street and gathered on the front lawn which overlooked a lake. It was an event.

I remember coming up out of the water. Just like a newborn baby I gasped for that first breath. I was new. I had a new identity, the old had passed away. Something powerful had happened.

In my forty plus years of serving the Lord I have only baptized one person, a young girl. As I pulled her up out of the water, I felt something. I felt God's power released. The Holy Spirit was on her, and He received her.

I used to think baptism was a sign to unbelievers but now I think differently. I believe it is a birth, into a new life. Now don't get me wrong and think I am saying you are not saved without baptism, I'm not. I am saying something happens, something good.

Becoming Who We Were Created to Be

God has restored our identity through Jesus. In Him we have been set free from the twisted selfish identity that looks like Satan and we are free to be what we were created in God's image to be.

Our identity changes when we come to the Lord. Before I came to the Lord my identity was worthlessness, nothing mattered. I felt empty. I was not true to anyone, and I was not true to myself. Whatever happened to me I told myself it did not matter, and I lived accordingly. I would not have lived long if I had not gotten saved.

So, what is this new identity? Who are we? What is different?

Our identity is so glorious and so wonderful it is beyond belief. Our identity is that we are loved.

I saw a movie in high school, many years ago called *Johnny Lingo*. The story took place in the Polynesian Islands. Johnny Lingo was the hero of the islands because he had become a great trader. Johnny Lingo comes home to his home island to bargain for a wife. The whole island is alive in excitement because the great Johnny Lingo was coming.

In this culture the husband to be, had to bargain with the father of his bride with cows. The common price for a wife was three cows, but a very high-priced wife was five cows.

Johnny Lingo had come to bargain with a greedy selfish man for his daughter Mahana.

Mahana was considered ugly and worthless by everyone on the island. Everyone on the island could not understand why Johnny Lingo wanted Mahana for a wife. They speculated that maybe the reason was the great trader would try to get a wife for only one cow, a great bargain.

As Johnny Lingo arrives on the island all the people gather around to see what he does. He comes to Mahana's father and sits down to bargain. All the townspeople have gathered to watch. Mahana is watching from a tree.

She stays in hiding because she is the laughingstock of the island. Her hair is unkempt, and she rarely looks up but keeps her head hung down in shame. Her father has told her she is not even worth one cow. Everyone thinks she is undesirable. She thinks Johnny is just making sport of her.

Johnny and Mahana's father sit down to bargain and Johnny asks him how much he wants for his daughter. Mahana's father thinks she is worthless, but he is greedy, and

he demands three cows for her. Everyone present laughs at his greed knowing he will never get three cows for such a worthless woman. But to everyone's surprise Johnny Lingo says he would never pay such a low price for Mahana. She is worth too much. Then Johnny says he will pay eight cows!
Eight cows! Such a high price has never been paid for a bride!

Johnny says he will be back later that day with the cows. Mahana's greedy father rubs his hands together with glee for he is now going to be rich and rid himself of his worthless daughter. As the father waits for Johnny's return with the cows Mahana cries out, "He will not return, he was fooling you."

But Johnny returns with the eight cows. He finds Mahana hiding behind the door. She is forlorn and ragged looking, but he lovingly takes her hand and leads her out. Johnny takes his new bride away from the island for a lengthy honeymoon and the two do not return for many months.

When they return home Mahana is a different woman. Everyone gasps when they see her. She is beautiful and confident. She appears in a beautiful dress with flowers in her hair. She has a new identity. She is radiant.

What has happened to Mahana?

She is loved and she is cherished. She is the wife of the hero, Johnny Lingo. She is the only wife who was ever bought with eight cows. Johnny declares he had loved her since they had been children and she had always been beautiful to him.

Mahana had received a new identity because of the great value placed on her by her husband. He gladly gave his riches to attain her because he loved her so.

We also have received a new identity. Our new identity is very similar to Mahana's but on a much, much higher scale.

148

We have been paid for with an unbelievable price. Our worth is astounding.

All of God's creation stood in wonder and amazement, when their Creator, their King, their God gave His all for lowly fallen man. He left heaven and put off His deity and became human. Then in utter humility he suffered and submitted Himself to torture not only from humans but also from fallen angels. All of God's mighty angels and magnificent beings stood back and watched in utter horror as Jesus allowed Himself to be shredded and tortured, mocked and spit upon and then dragged by Satan to the lowest pit in the underworld and put through the most extreme hell.

What could possibly be worth so much?

What did God see in these lowly fallen beings?

How could God pay such an unthinkable high price?

How could the Spirit of God actually live inside of them?

Our new Identity is loved. We are loved by God, the Father, the Son and the Holy Spirit! He has emptied Himself for us because He puts such a high value on us.

What does this mean?

It means our identity is in His love. It means that we have such a high value that we can see ourselves in a whole new light. Our worth is so high that our worth now is unshakeable and unmovable.

When our identity becomes that we are loved [by God]] then we become love. We begin to look just like Him, we look like love and our lives begin to shine. We begin to love like we have been loved.

We are no longer moved by the hatred others.............

Because we are so loved by God.

We no longer have to defend ourselves, ever...we can

be at peace no matter what...

Because we are so loved by God.

We live for one reason alone, Him,

He is with us,

He will never leave us,

He is living inside of us, His life is our life.

Has anyone ever lived like this before? Yes, Jesus did, of course, but others have too. Let's look at Stephen in the Bible, the first martyr.

Stephen the Bible tells us was a man full of faith and power and that he did great wonders and signs among the people. Some men rose up against Stephen and tried to dispute him, but they got nowhere because of the wisdom and the Spirit by which Stephen spoke. When these religious men could not bring down Stephen by logic, they resorted lies and brought false charges against him.

Stephen gets hauled into court. Now in court Stephen boldly speaks the truth. The truth enrages the religious leaders, and they gnash their teeth at him and take Stephen out and stone him. As they are stoning Stephen his last words are a prayer for those who are killing him.

Nowhere in this story is Stephen responding like a normal human. Stephen is responding like a mature son of God. This is our goal. His identity is no longer in himself; Stephen's identity is in Christ, and he looks like Christ. Not only is Stephen doing great miracles of faith, {Faith works by love] Stephen is unmovable. He did not run and hide, and he did not back down, he proclaimed only truth even unto death and he died praying for his enemies, one of which was Paul who got saved soon after.

Stephen's secret is his identity is in Christ. He is now

unmovable, like Christ. Everything God does is for man's redemption, and this is the same with Stephen. His whole motivation, just like God has become love. Stephen never tries to defend himself. Stephen never tried to save his own life and Stephen was not angry with the people who were throwing rocks at him until he died.

Stephen has attained the measure of the stature of the fullness of Christ. His identity was so rooted in God's love he became love, and he responded just like Jesus. Is it possible to actually live like this?

This is our goal to live like this.

It is Satan's goal to keep you from living like this and if you do, he will persecute like he did Stephen. But Satan could not defeat Stephen and it is no coincidence that Satan took a terrible blow in his kingdom. Satan's top man, Paul who is persecuting the church and had his part in Stephen's death soon changes camps. Read the Book of Acts, Stephen is martyred in chapter seven and Paul is saved in chapter nine.

Is Stephen's story over? No, Stephen's story has just begun. Stephen will rule and reign with Christ for eons to come in eternity because he has become a son of God. Not every believer achieves that status, many are just content with making it into heaven, and they will. But they will not rule and reign with Christ, it will be on a much lower level.

Believe me Satan wants to keep you from your identity in Christ. He cannot touch you if you find your true identity. He did not defeat Stephen, Stephen defeated him.

If you find your identity in Christ does that mean you will be martyred?

Every disciple was martyred except John, and they tried to kill him, he just didn't die. And just like Jesus no one died

151

before their time, many walked away from death, Paul was stoned, and they thought he was dead, but he got up and walked away. You may not be martyred but if you are, you will be ready; you will be unmovable when you find your true identity in Christ.

Chapter Twenty

NO MORE BAD ATTITUDES

Being created in God's image carries huge responsibility. We are creative beings with power. Of course, God cannot trust us with much power at this time or we would totally annihilate each other, but still, we have power.

I actually have gone through my whole life ignorant of this and now I am only beginning to see how important my thoughts and attitudes are. Our thoughts and attitudes have force. They actually have an effect on us and the people around us.

The first little inkling I got of this was in a situation at work. I got a new supervisor. At first, I really liked her.

Then she did some things I really did not like. Then she did a couple of other things I did not like. One time she humiliated me in front of a patient. Now I did not like her at all. But she was my supervisor, so I put on a fake smile when I saw her and did my best to pretend, after all I did not want trouble with my job.

The Lord showed me that that would not work. I could be pleasant to her face, but my attitude was something real in the spirit realm. She was a spirit, and I am a spirit. There was no way I could hide this bad attitude. Even though I did nothing face to face with her to show her I did not like her, I was releasing a force.

Wow, that got me thinking. I can be as fake as fake can be and I thought I was getting away with it. I have to deal with my attitudes! I thought I could hide them and behave well and that would be enough. It is not!

Thoughts and attitudes are very real. Neville Johnson, a marvelous, anointed minister from Australia teaches about this. Neville had a period in his life when God opened the spiritual realm to him. It was very hard for him, and he asked God to please make it stop. But Neville could actually see that certain thoughts and attitudes actually emit colors and smells in the spiritual realm. He said everyone emits light, but those who have bad attitudes such as self-pity emit a dinghy, dark light that is also putrid. Each negative attitude has its own bad color and smell, jealousy has one, hatred has one etc.

They also have a vibration. This can negatively affect the health of the person and also the atmosphere around them. It also attracts negative spirits and trouble.

Of course, the opposite is also true. Positive attitudes such as love, joy, peace have a beautiful color and a beautiful smell. They emit a different vibration and attract angels and repel demons. They also positively affect those around them.

This started the wheels turning in my head. I had a lot of changing to do. I realized something else. How other people feel about me emits a power toward me. Other people have power. I don't want them releasing negative power my way. This made me realize I need to do even more changing. I needed to be careful how I treat strangers.

Maybe I should not try to beat people out of a better parking spot or get ahead of someone in line at the grocery store. Maybe I need to be kind and considerate to everyone, even strangers. I need to put out good, so I don't reap negative power against me.

I realized I need to live more carefully because I am created in God's image. And so are all the rest of these people on this planet, we affect each other!

I had to try this the other day. I was about to turn into a good parking space, it was one of those days that the whole parking lot was full. Just before I turned in another car came up the opposite way looking for a space. I waited and then waved him in. They looked happy and gave me a thank you wave. They actually blessed me. Even though it was a small thing, they have power and they blessed me, I know because immediately my shopping trip became almost supernatural.

As I continued down the lot toward the store a car pulled out of the first spot. I actually parked in the first spot! The only way that ever happens is if I shop at 5am and even then, it is rare. I gave a little shriek of delight, thinking it had something to do with being blessed by a stranger.

It continued, I got to the deli department and there were no numbers, the number machine was broken. There was a mob in front of the deli trying to get waited on. I was scanning the deli for a few minutes and then looked up at the crowd and wondered how I would ever get waited on. They were waiting on people by yelling who is next and the process was going very slow. I had forgotten to look at the crowd and I had no idea when my turn would be. I thought this will take forever, but when the young man behind the deli counter shouted, "Who's next?"

An older man shouted out, "She is!" while pointing at me.

I thought, "I am still getting blessed! But it wasn't over yet when I arrived at the checkout lanes the lines were ridiculous. I thought I was in for another long wait, but as I was passing a closed lane the cashier called me in and opened the lane. I had no waiting.

God was teaching me something. He was teaching me that we humans are created in His image and when even strangers bless us or curse us it has power. I needed to be careful how I treated strangers. I never was before.

I remember hearing a woman preacher speak one time and what she said shocked me. She was talking about how she had four children and she had never had trouble during her pregnancies, until the last one. She was sick, sick sick. She wondered why, so she prayed about it. What the Lord showed her shocked her. She had been critical of a woman who was in her prayer meeting who did not show up during her pregnancy because she said she didn't feel good. That attitude of judgement came back on herself! She was sick because she had judged the woman who had been sick!

Oh, my goodness am I in trouble!!!!!! I do rotten stuff like that all the time! I have got to change! No more bad attitudes!

No more harsh words!

No more faking it, I need to be sincere and truly love people.

No more push and shove.

I have to be alert and kind to those around me, even strangers.

I am created in God's image, my words carry power, my thoughts carry power, my attitudes carry power! I am shaping and creating my world! I am shaping and creating in the world of those around me!

Believe me there are times I don't want to get back what I am sending out! I don't want to reap what I am sowing!

But What about Troublemakers?

I talked about how other people's attitudes toward us can cause us trouble because they are releasing a force toward us. There are some people that will not like us no matter what. They are trouble and they make trouble wherever they go.

I have a friend who has a daughter-in law like that. She is at war with the world. This girl is trouble everywhere she goes. She starts trouble at work, she starts trouble with her so-called friends, and she starts trouble in her family. She goes around telling lies about people and she stirs up trouble. She is an extreme case.

How do we handle situations like that?

Very carefully. It is best not to be around people like that but if like my friend it cannot be avoided it can be very hard. But it can be done. I was in a situation like that. You cannot get pulled into a grudge. You cannot allow another person to spoil your attitude.

God actually considers these people to be in witchcraft. You are dealing with a witchcraft spirit, even though sometimes the person is a Christian. It can be a real battle. I had this happen to me and the Lord helped me through it.

I let a woman come and live with me who needed a place to stay. She was a Christian, sort of. She was trouble and she made trouble everywhere she went. She upset my household. Even though she went to church and talked about God, she was operating under witchcraft.

The Lord instructed me to find one good thing about her and dwell on that. It was hard but I thought of something. I kept my mind fixed on her one good thing and I changed my attitude. It broke the power of witchcraft over me.

If someone is causing you trouble in the spiritual realm this way, you cannot fall for the trap. Try what the Lord told me. You break the power of evil by not letting it infect you. Stay in the good in your thoughts and attitudes. God always has an answer and love always overcomes evil. That's what God does, and we are created in His image. If it works for Him, it will work for us.

No more bad attitudes!

Chapter Twenty-One

NEW WINESKINS

The disciples of John and of the Pharisees were fasting. Then they came and said to Him, "Why do the disciples of John and of the Pharisees fast, but Your disciples do not fast,

And Jesus said to them, "Can the friends of the bridegroom fast while the bridegroom is with them? As long as they have the bridegroom with them, they cannot fast. But the days will come when the bridegroom will be taken away from them, and they will fast in those days.

No one sews a piece of unshrunk cloth on an old garment; or else the new piece pulls away from the old, and the tear is made worse. And no one puts new wine into old wineskins; or else the new wine bursts the wineskins; the wine is spilled, and the wineskins are ruined. But the new wine must be put onto new wineskins." Mark 2:18-22

My sister Carol, my daughter Joy and I get together weekly to pray. They are exciting times; we never know what to expect. Each week is different, and each week God has something new up His sleeve for us. This week was no different. We started off to pray but we kept talking instead. We started to pray again when Joy said, "Do you want to hear what the Lord has been teaching me this week about the new wineskins?"

"Yes," I said because I knew if the Lord was teaching her about a certain scripture it had to be good.

"Well," Joy began explaining, "When John's disciples asked Jesus why His disciples did not fast, Jesus told them the time would come when they would fast and then He started talking about the wineskins.

"The disciples were not yet ready to fast they had just recently begun following Jesus. They probably could not have done it, I mean, they could not even stay awake and pray with Jesus for one hour, they all fell asleep.

"When Jesus talks about the wineskins He is talking about our minds being renewed. The disciples' minds had to be renewed first. We can't move on to a new thing with an old mind set, and that is true with anything. Like say...," Joy thought for a moment, "even a diet. If you go on a diet unprepared and go on buying the same old junk food, you will end up eating more, you just make things worse."

Joy continued, "If the Lord were to pour in the new thing, He is doing into us before our mind is renewed then it would just make things worse, the wine skins would tear. The time came when the disciples did fast and more, they even

160

suffered for the Lord, but they were prepared, their minds had been renewed."

My ears perked up as Joy was talking because as she explained things I was thinking about my own life. I knew God was trying to get me to think differently about my finances, and not just my finances the whole struggling to survive thing, but I just wasn't getting it. Now I was realizing as Joy was talking that God had been trying to renew my mind in that area, but my old mindset was hanging on and it just would not break.

You see, I went from a stay-at-home mother to the breadwinner or sometimes co bread winner about twenty-three years ago. For normal people that should not be all that big of a deal but for me it has been heavy, very heavy. Neither I nor my husband are very good at making money. So, I did two things.

Number one, I have worked many hours of overtime or worked extra jobs on the side, for years {yeeeeaaarrrss] to try to make ends meet. Or the only time I would call in sick was if I were so ill, I had to go into the hospital. In other words, I am worn to a frazzle. This is not working for me anymore because my body is getting old.

Number two, I became very cheap. I cut coupons, I scour the grocery ads for the lowest prices, and I am very good at getting things free. A lot of groceries stores have rules if they charge you the wrong price the item is free. I got so I could spot a wrong price a mile away. I got loads of things free.

Then in Michigan we have what is called the scan law. If the wrong price scans and you pay it, you can go to the help desk and not only get the amount over you paid back, but you also get five dollars back. I did it every time I shopped. I knew the price of everything, and I could spot a wrong price tag in a second.

Oh, but I was even cheaper than that. {I say was, I think I still am} I would go to garage sales to get the things I need, furniture, bedding clothes, kitchenware, etc. I never pay the price people put on their stuff; I always offer half. If they won't dicker with the price, I go on to the next garage sale. I am the queen of cheap.

Oh, I have other tricks too. I have the credit card with the highest rewards, and I pay all my bills with it so I can get the most money back. Actually, I have two credit cards that I use to get the maximum rewards possible. My husband is always calling me from the grocery store or the gas station and saying, "Which credit card am I supposed to use here, the red one or the blue one?"

Every little bit helps right?

And you know I would never buy a lottery ticket, right? I don't believe in because it is gambling, but I would enter in contests because that wasn't gambling and then I would beg God to make me the winner. I could not figure out why I didn't win, I was just trying to make God's job of providing for me easier.

Well, the first thing to go was the scan law at the store. That was a couple of years ago. I asked God if it was okay with Him if I was doing that. He said I was being crafty.

Uh oh.... I did not like that word. That was the word used to describe the serpent in the garden that tricked Eve into eating from the tree.

So, I told God I would not deliberately get the scan law.

More things came up. I had entered a small contest and the prize was three thousand dollars. I knew that that amount would help me catch up on bills and God wants us to pay our bills, right? I was so sure I was going to win that I waited impatiently for the day of the contest.

I did not win.

I did some talking to God, after all someone had to win, why not me?

In His way of communicating, He somehow let me know He did not want me to enter contests anymore, He wanted me to look only to Him and not contests. It seemed easier to me if I just would win the contest, but I wanted to please God, so, I stopped entering contests.

Then, just this year I felt like God was dealing with me to pay off some medical bills that I had in collections. I had finally paid off the ones that had not gone into collections and I was tired of all my money going to medical bills. Now, He wanted me to get working on the ones in collections. I had a better idea, I wanted to pay off my second mortgage and just let those other bills sit for a while longer.

Nope.

Well then, I came up with a great plan. I was approved for a new credit card that would pay me $200. In rewards after I spent $1000. Plus, if I changed banks, I could get another $300 for switching. That would be $500 toward my debts, which were about $1300. But every time I prayed about doing that, I did not get a good feeling. Finally, I asked Joy to pray with me about it and she said, "I don't think you can. God never lets me do finagling stuff like that either."

She used the words finagling. That word did not sit good with me either. I didn't change banks or apply for the credit card. Somehow, I managed to pay of my debts without any tricks, but God did provide extra money I had no idea was coming.

But I have been praying about finances more than ever. I have been pulling on God in prayer. I need more income, every month is a struggle, and I am too tired for lots of overtime, and that is, if I can get it.

Now, here's Joy talking about new wineskins. Suddenly I realized God wants to get me ready for something new in this area, but my mind has to be renewed. My problem is not bills and money, my problem is these old wineskins. God wants to do something new in my life, but He can't just yet. I have to let go of my old way of thinking. I need my mind renewed when it comes to money, and life and struggle. I need to think like God thinks in this area. I need to get in my Bible and get these old ideas broken.

I suddenly realize there are prayers I pray that God cannot answer because of me. Yes, He has kept us going and He provides for me, but He is wanting to do something new, and I have to get ready. This is about God's kingdom come and God's will be done, and not about easy life for Summer. I have to think differently about all of it. He can't answer these prayers because they are prayed out wrong attitudes and mindsets that have to go.

New wineskins do not just have to do with finances. New wineskins have to do with God doing something in your life and you have to be ready, no matter what it is.

Look at the change that happened in the disciples. They were not the same men they used to be. These were the ones that fought over who would be the greatest or wanted to call fire down from heaven to devour a city. God changed the way they thought. They were prepared for the new things God had planned for them. They were ready because their minds were

164

renewed, and their wineskins were new. God could trust them with power, great power.

What happened to Peter? The one who cut off someone's ear with a sword, the one who denied Jesus three times, the one who told Jesus that He wouldn't die on a cross, and Jesus rebuked him. Peter has changed and God is doing a new thing in him. Peter pulled up a beggar who was lame and he began walking and leaping. Peter's shadow would fall on someone, and they would be healed. Peter is defying the Pharisees and preaching boldly. But it is not just Peter; all the disciples are doing new things.

Phillip would teleport from one place to another and wherever he went he preached and rejoiced. They all preached and performed miracles around the then known world, traveling far and wide and doing wonders. And all but John were bravely martyred, and that was only because when they tried to kill him, he wouldn't die.

This thing God wants to do in us, these changes He wants to make. They have to do with a new and different mindset, and it is not selfish and self-centered or prideful or greedy or fearful, like my financial mindset. No, none of these men were any longer fearful.

It is said Peter asked to be crucified upside down because he was not worthy to die like Jesus. Andrew was scourged and crucified, and he hung on a cross for two days preaching to those who passed by. Thomas was killed in India with a spear. John was boiled in oil.

No, new mind sets are not for those who want to live like the world and live for themselves. They are for those who want to live and think and be like Christ. Those who want the new wine to flow through them.

New mindsets come from the word of God, and from following the Holy Spirits leading and being taught by Him. It is hard to let go of the old wineskins, the old and comfortable way of thinking. It goes against our carnal nature. But I want to be ready for the next and new thing God wants to do. I want new wineskins and new wine.

After Joy finished telling us about what God was teaching her, we got quiet and started to pray.

"Okay God," I said "I want to change, please help me to let go of my conniving and finagling and my fear. I want to do things Your way, please get me ready for the new thing you want to do in me."

Chapter Twenty-Two

IT'S BETWEEN YOU AND GOD

We have already talked somewhat about God's attention to detail. He knows you completely and intimately. He sees you down to every cell, molecule and atom of your body. He has very intricately designed your DNA. Jesus said the very hairs of our heads were numbered. He knows your every thought and motive of your heart. He has whole books written and recorded about you, in heaven, and one is a detailed plan for your life. His plan goes way beyond these short years you will live on this earth, they go forward eons into eternity. He is a God of detail, extreme detail. He planned every day of your life, way before you were born, before He created the earth to put you in.

So...keeping that in mind, what about these details in your life? Let's stop looking at everything horizontally and let's start looking at everything vertically. In other words, keep everything between you and God. This means that how you respond to the situations and the people in your life is about you and God, believing that He is intimately involved in your life and how you respond has eternal importance. How do we do this?

Well, I started in my marriage. My marriage is more between me and God than me and my husband. It had to be, or I wouldn't have had a marriage, {Thus the title of my first book, *The Impossible Marriage*}. It was not possible to deal with issues with my husband. I would try to talk to him about how devastating his drinking was to me.

Devastating is an understatement. I had an unnatural fear of being around someone who had been drinking. Just to smell it on their breath would paralyze me with fear and I would feel myself shut down and want to curl up and die. {It had to do with the past and a pedophile stepfather} Not to mention my husband Jim was a mean drunk. I felt the biggest need in my life was for Jim to stop drinking immediately. I tried to reason with Jim. Jim would agree with me. He would look me in the eye and promise me that he would never ever drink again; he'd say that he hated that stuff! It might last a couple days or maybe just hours or maybe even minutes. My torture would begin again.

There was no way to deal with Jim, it became between me and God. God did not have it easy. I came to Him with fear and anger, rage and confusion. He'd let me rail, "I am leaving him I hate him! I can't stand this another minute!!!!!!!"

Sometimes God also got the brunt of my wrath for not changing things. It was between us. I have screamed and yelled and sworn at God. He never held it against me. But ultimately, how I responded was between me and God. I needed it to be, and God was willing. He was always there through everything we went through.

If there is a person in your life that it is impossible to deal with, every effort to deal with them ends in fights or hurt feelings. Stop dealing with them. Deal with God instead. He will tell you how to respond and what your part will be.

God had plans for my relationship with Jim. He began to tell me what to do and how to respond. He began to reveal to me why Jim was behaving like he was and showing me what was really going on. He began to speak to me on a regular basis, even sometimes in supernatural ways, through dreams, visions, even sometimes audibly or through angels. I was not in this marriage alone I was in it with God, and He was coming through for me.

He even gave me promises regarding my marriage, promises that were impossible that required miracles to fulfill. My marriage became supernatural. Supernatural because the God of the universe was committed to it, because my marriage was about God and me, {Jim too of course.} I began to realize just how much God loved Jim and He wanted to show Jim love through me, because love was something Jim knew very little about.

God's purpose for my marriage was to bring healing to both Jim and I, through love and forgiveness. It was to bring both of us closer to Him and to grow us up. It was to create the image of His Son on the inside of us, two broken, immature and shattered people. God required me over and over to love and forgive.

Sometimes what God required of me seemed just too hard and I did not think I could do it, but I had no choice, I just did it because I could not handle my marriage without God. Like the time God told me I actually had to leave my husband.

After all those years of threatening God that I would leave Jim, I really, really did not want to leave Jim. Obeying God on that one was the hardest thing I ever had to do.

Sometimes I had to stand up to Jim, God required it. That was scary, standing up to an angry, alcoholic, ex-convict who could fight four men at once and send them all to the hospital. {that really happened] Jim was not easy to stand up too. That is when God sent an angel to help me.

Sometimes the hardest part was just overcoming my own rage. I learned I could not repress it, I had to get rid of it, and there was plenty of it to get rid of. God helped me with that too.

God has been so faithful to me in my marriage it takes my breath away. One of the biggest promises God gave me was that my husband would not go back to prison. Jim had been incarcerated or on probation or parole since he was a young teen. He did not stay out of trouble for long. Jim has been arrested for several felonies since we were married. Each time he faced long prison sentences, but each time God fulfilled His promise. No one could figure out how Jim was getting so many breaks.

My marriage, though difficult, has become my testimony, my testimony of God's faithfulness. I know if you have read many of my books you have heard all of this before, but I never tire of telling it. My marriage has also become my healing. My marriage was absolutely impossible, until it became between God and me.

Just recently, I realized, everything can be between God and me, not just my marriage. We do not have to engage in conflict with people. Some people or situations you cannot deal with without conflict. Don't. Deal with God instead.

My daughter and I were not getting along too well for a while. She had moved back home as an adult and the lines of who is in charge were kind of blurry, sometimes. But our real problem was her car insurance.

Lonna had moved home to help her sister, Joy, who was going through nursing school. Joy was now a single mother, recently divorced, with three small children and in her last fourteen months of nursing college which was very demanding. Her last year would take her all over the state to different hospitals and she would be gone sometimes for days. This would not have been possible for her to do except for her older sister Lonna moved back from Arizona to Michigan and put her own life on hold to babysit Joy's children, for free.

Of course, she moved in with Jim and I, and we helped her by paying for her car insurance for her. I was amazed at Lonna's sacrifice she had made for her sister and the well-being of her children.

After Joy finished school, it was Lonna's time to try to figure out what to do with her own life, she had recently been divorced also. She stayed home with us, and she was still on my car insurance, but I now required her to pay it, especially since she had a little fender bender in a parking lot and suddenly our car insurance soared.

Lonna is really kind of a free thinker. She never worries about anything, and she didn't seem to worry about her car insurance, I mean getting it paid. Lonna seemed to be going through a couple of years of ups and downs, ups and downs with her life and ups and downs with her money. In the meantime, this was putting the pinch on me, financially. Eventually she enrolled in school part time and was working part time and things went smoothly for a while, until she quit

171

her job and started school full time. I was hoping she had some kind of plan to pay for her car insurance. She didn't.

A lot of people were happy to give me advice. "She's a grown woman, just cancel her car insurance and let her worry about it."

I was confused and I did not know what to do and every time I would try to talk to her it would end up in a shouting match. I was getting to the end of my rope; I did not know how to deal with her. I loved her but we weren't getting along.

Finally, I realized I could not deal with her. It wasn't working. I said, "I am not going to deal with her, I am going to make this between me and God."

I asked God what I should do. I told Him it was between me and Him, whatever He told me I would do. Even if He told me to pay it forever or if He told me not to pay it. At first, I did not know what He wanted. He didn't answer right away. I kept praying and waiting. Then God revealed to me that Lonna was under a lot of pressure and stress, and she felt very alone. That was a revelation because Lonna puts on a good confident front.

This was November and my current policy ended mid-December. Suddenly I knew what I was supposed to do. I just knew. I was supposed to take her off my policy but pay for a couple of months for her on her own new policy, to give her time to find a job and get money without adding to the pressure she was feeling. I felt such joy and peace about knowing God's plan. I wondered how Lonna would feel. When I told her, she seemed pleased.

Praise the Lord! We were communicating and getting along! And it was all because God knew exactly what to do. But God had a big surprise up His gigantic sleeve for me, it got even better.

My other daughter Joy had just gotten a new insurance agent she was happy with. She wanted me to call her before I renewed my car insurance with my company. So, I did, I had her quote a price for me and also one for Lonna's car insurance. She found us a different company with the exact same coverage for less than half of what I was currently paying and almost exactly half of what Lonna was currently paying! I could not believe it!

I felt like a million pounds had rolled off my back! Not only was this a major breakthrough in my finances it was a major breakthrough in my relationship with my daughter. We were enjoying each other again. When I make things between me and God, He does things better than I could possibly imagine.

God does not want us to engage in human conflict. He always has a better answer. He can discern a situation correctly and help us do the right thing. I do not have to deal with impossible people and situations. I can do things a better way. I can make it between me and God!

I had another experience learning this lesson that happened many years ago when my husband lost the best job he had ever had. Jim had been working as a waiter in a good restaurant for seven years. It was just the right fit for him job wise. He had regular customers that had been coming to eat in his section for years and he made enough money that I did not have to work.

Everything went fine until that company that owned the restaurant chain sent a new man in to change things. He got rid of the managers that had worked there since the restaurant opened and every day, he fired someone else.

Finally, Jim's day came, he was fired. We were all devastated. This job had meant an end to poverty for us and here it was again.

We were immediately in trouble, so I went to apply for food stamps. That is when I found out how mean and heartless this man who fired everyone at the restaurant really was. At the food stamp office, they had to verify that Jim really was fired and didn't quit. So, I gave the social worker the phone number to the restaurant so she could call and verify it. She called me back at home and said this man had told her Jim quit. When I reaffirmed, he hadn't quit she told me to go into the restaurant and get this man to write a note that he had fired and Jim and bring it to her.

I went into the restaurant to talk with this guy. He was awful. He refused to sign the note and he also denied telling the social worker that Jim had quit. He was an evil man, and he was enjoying making trouble for people and he was enjoying making trouble for me. He smirked at me and sent me out the door.

I did not know what to do. We had a family of five and no food.

The Lord told me, not to struggle with this man. He told me to just drop the whole thing and forget the food stamps.

So, I obeyed the Lord and did nothing, and we struggled along. This was in December. In January Jim applied for a job working in the kitchen at Tiger Town. This was where the Detroit Tiger baseball team trained in the winter. Jim, being from Detroit himself hit it off immediately with the kitchen manager and was immediately hired. The pay was not good but there was a fringe benefit.

FOOD!

Because they cooked wonderful food for these pro-ball players and they did not feed them leftovers, the leftovers came home with Jim. We did not just get food, we got delicious, prepared food like we had never eaten in our lives. Swiss steak and mashed potatoes, salads and fish and straw berry shortcakes, and you name it we got it. Jim would even bring home whole gallons of milk that were about to go out of date.   Jim brought home so much food that we could not eat it all he even was bringing some to our next-door neighbor's house. We all gained weight, we couldn't help it we were eating like kings, {pro ball player kings}.

It actually took me awhile to put it together that God did this because of the food stamp thing. He was rewarding our obedience not to struggle with this evil man. I think there was another reason also He did not want us to struggle with this man; He allows people the free will to choose evil.

This man chose evil, and it caused us to suffer, and we did suffer. We went for about six weeks barely eating. But He does punish sin. That restaurant chain, which was a popular restaurant in the south, went out of business shortly after. We had moved back to Michigan by that time, but a new restaurant chain took over the very same spot and many of the old employees were hired by the new restaurant.

Again, we can stop dealing horizontally and engaging in conflict with people, because if we do, we will get caught up in all kinds of trouble and hurt and pain. We can make situations about us and God. The more we learn to do this the better our lives will be.

Chapter Twenty-Three

THE HIGH CALLING

Brethren, I count not myself to have apprehended: but this one thing I do, forgetting those things which are behind, and reaching forth to those things which are before,
I press toward the mark for the prize of the high calling of God in Christ Jesus. Philippians 3:13-14

What is this high calling we are called to? This high calling that Paul was pressing toward so desperately. All through the New Testament the believers were pressing toward this goal, this prize, they were willing to face anything to obtain it.

I want to talk about this, the Bible only gives us a peek, so let's peek. The High Calling has to do with the eons of eternity to come and ruling and reigning with Christ.

Ruling and reigning what?
Uh, the universe!
Have you ever gone out on a dark summer night and

looked up at the sky? There are billions and billions of stars and planets and solar systems and galaxies. There are so many it boggles the human brain. God has plans for all that you know. He has plans in the future but first He is getting together His staff, His kings and priests. The rulers of this universe to come are being called and trained now on this planet called earth. Many are called but only a few will be chosen, those who overcome in this life.

This earthly life is a testing ground. A testing ground to prove who is worthy, who is faithful and who has the character to be found able to rule with God. He has created us in His image. He has called us to become His children and He has called some, the overcomers, to the High Calling, to rule and reign with Him.

The book of Revelation takes us through a progression of events; events that are yet to come. The exciting news is these events have begun and we are in the final chapter of the world as we know it and the world as we know it is about to change.

A final move of God is coming on the earth. Millions will come to the Lord. Jesus will restore all things through us His body. The believers on earth will begin to walk in the powers of the age to come. There will be no more grey areas. The world and the followers of Satan will become vile beyond belief and we the body of Christ will become lighter and lighter. The Bible says, *Arise, shine, for thy light is come and the glory of the Lord is risen upon thee. For, behold, the darkness shall cover the earth, and gross darkness the people; but the Lord shall arise upon thee, and His glory shall be seen on thee. Isaiah 60:1-2*

Then Satan and all evil will have their last hurrah. They will actually try to overthrow God but that will be a very short and deadly battle. Satan's human followers will immediately be cast into the lake of fire and Satan will be bound and cast onto the bottomless pit for one thousand years.

The Millennium

This will begin the thousand-year reign of Christ from the world's capital city Jerusalem. There will not be any more atheists at this time because God will clearly be seen. Jesus will rule the earth, and He will rule it with an iron scepter. That means we won't be having a sin problem.

This will be a wonderful time to live on earth! It will be a time when there will be two kinds of people on the earth. Some will be in their normal mortal bodies, and some will have resurrected bodies. Remember the rapture will have already happened.

Not every believer will have the privilege of ruling with Christ on earth during the millennium. They have to qualify, only those who have proved themselves worthy in this training ground called life. They are called overcomers.

We are constantly facing tests during our lifetime. They are tests that will determine whether we prove worthy of the High calling of Christ. Those who prove worthy are not necessarily those who did great exploits but those who have put on humility, and those who have developed the character of Christ. Those who have become like Him. This is our true test in life. The rewards are more than we can possibly imagine at this time.

This is why we do not see God. This is why we are tested sometimes beyond endurance, like Job was, like Paul was, or Joseph or Abraham or those we find in the Hall of Faith in Hebrews chapter twelve. This is why we are to rejoice in our trials because of the glory that follows.

This fallen world is the ultimate testing ground. There is nothing quite like it in the universe or will there ever be again. A place of where darkness and evil exist, and we can only see the beauty of God dimly through the eyes of faith. A place where we can actually choose to deny ourselves and take up an invisible cross and chose to suffer with Christ. It is a privilege and an honor to be chosen to be where we are. We have a chance for the High calling. Let me say that again, "You have a chance for the High Calling!"

It isn't easy.

Paul was pressing in for the High Calling.

Nature Restored During the Millennium

The millennium will be an incredible time where nature will be restored. The animals will not be dangerous. This is mentioned in Isaiah *11:6 The wolf also shall dwell with the lamb, and the leopard shall lie down with the kid; and the calf and the young lion and the fatling together; and the lion shall eat straw like the ox. And the suckling child shall play on the hole of the asp, and the weaned child shall put his hand on the cockatrice den. KJV*

When Adam was in the Garden of Eden, he had authority over every atom and molecule. His words could command and create an atmosphere of heaven. The animals were under his loving care, and he could communicate with them. We know this because Eve had a conversation with the serpent. This was not strange to her. We did not eat animals and animals did not eat each other.

The weather was not violent. There were no storms or foul weather. The earth was at peace. This will be restored. Nature and man will be at peace again. There will be no more wild animals. There will be no earthquakes and hurricanes or tornados. The earth will be a beautiful place like it was meant to be.

Neville Johnson in his sermon the Bigger Picture tells of seeing into the future, into the millennium. He talks of seeing incredible things. He said the rebuilding of the earth would be half human effort and half supernatural. He saw beautiful cities that's architecture was indescribable. He saw different technology, cars that did not touch the ground and received energy from another source. He saw huge aircraft that could move huge amounts of people because once a year everyone goes to Jerusalem. He saw many things that he did not even understand. It will be an incredible time. A new world is soon coming! It is a world beyond your imagination where His will is done on earth as it is in heaven. We have prayed for this for centuries.

For those who are chosen to live and reign with Christ for a thousand years during the millennium period, they will have entered another training ground. They are being prepared for even greater things. According to Neville earth will one day be the capital of the universe! Remember we have eons to come. What will we be doing? We have a chance for the High Calling.

The Greatest Hour

Neville also talks in his sermons about how blessed we are to have been chosen to be here. He means here on this planet, at this time. He is trying to convey something huge, something other worldly something hard to understand. Then he describes his experience before the throne and seeing the little spirits that exist in the Father, us, and they are saying, "Send me, send me, I want to be a redeemed person send me."

And the Neville says, "And you were chosen."

Then Neville tries to convey how this fallen planet, Earth, is God's focus. How this troubled fallen planet is the perfect atmosphere to develop God's heroes.

Yes, the stakes are higher here on earth; millions and billions of souls are lost and slip into an eternity of hell. The stakes are higher, but the rewards are higher for those who overcome. You see evil will be done away with and there will not be another situation quite like this ever again. In the eons to come the overcomers will be the heroes of old. Because things will have changed, evil will have been dealt with. There will no longer be the opportunity to choose to live for Christ under such strong opposition.

And not only are we a spirit sent to this earth; we have been sent for this very hour. Neville says this is the greatest hour to be chosen to come. This is the end of the age. The greatest battles are just ahead, the greatest chances to overcome the greatest trials, the greatest chance to the greatest honor of all, the High Calling in Christ.

You see we will not all be equal in the next age. You choose your place. You choose how far or high you will go in

God. You choose by your life on earth, how you live. And remember it is not so much what you accomplish but what you become. We need to become like Jesus. Yes, God's work needs to be done, and it will be, but it is much more important what you become.

I think of Brother Lawrence a humble monk from the sixteenth century. He learned to fellowship continually with God. His duties were to wash dishes, and that is what he did. Many sought him out because of his close walk with the Lord but his life was lived humbly. It may have seemed that his life would not make much difference, but it has. After his death someone compiled the letters, he had written into a book which is still in print today. I have a copy it is called, *The Practice of the Presence of God.*

His book has been around for generations changing lives with his wisdom on companionship with God.

We will make a bigger impact on this world if we become like Christ rather than trying to pile up good works, because like in Brother Lawrence's case, it is God who multiplies the crumbs of our life and feeds them to the multitudes.

This goes against our thinking that as Christians we have to pile up works. I know I thought I had missed out as I watched the years go by and God had never used me in some magnificent way. But His will for me was to be a wife and a mother. I finally asked Him, "Are You ever going to use me?"

"Yes," He told me, "In the last move."

Look at Jesus' life. His ministry did not start until He was thirty years old, and He only lived to be thirty-three. God could have started using Him when he was twenty if He wanted to, but that was not His plan. In fact, had we lived in Jesus' time, and we did not have the New Testament to reveal to us the true purpose of Jesus death and resurrection, we might have thought His life was a failure, like everyone of that time thought. Even His disciples did not understand at first and thought all was lost.

Many victories are unseen. Many victories are spiritual victories. The kind of victories that no one knows about, but they change things in the real world, the spirit world, where the real battles take place that affect our world. Like when Jesus entered the underworld defeated Satan and returned to heaven with the keys to death, hell and the grave. Jesus had a ministry on earth, yes, but His greatest work was unseen by human eyes. His greatest work was our redemption.

Stephen, the first martyr's life was cut short, but his death was his victory. In his death he defeated Satan. It has to do with spiritual principles and justice. Patient suffering in our lives enacts a law of justice on our behalf which deals Satan a major blow. Stephens's death enacted great victories for the early church. Like Jesus, Stephen enacted something major in the invisible realm.

You may see your life and wonder, what is God doing?

He is using your life in the best way possible.

The Lord had to show me the major effect my husband's life had in the unseen realm. All I saw was Jim trying for years to fight his problems such as alcoholism, drug addictions and a tendency for trouble. He seemed to be failing for years on end. But that was not the case because as the Lord showed me, he never stopped fighting and he never stopped trying. His life of struggle was a major victory that no one could see. He has defeated Satan by not quitting and he has stood between Satan and his children and not allowed the curse of alcoholism to continue to his children as it had in his family lines for generations. My husband looks at his own life and sees failure because his victories are unseen by human eyes.

No matter what you are going through, do not quit. No matter how many times you fall, get back up. Remember, faithful, patient suffering enacts a principle that defeats Satan, and it is the principle of justice. God will never waste your suffering.

Suffering is one of the quickest ways to the higher calling, our goal and our highest reward. Humility is another. There are other ways too, obedience and patience, and of course love. The high calling is to be our mark, the goal we press forward to. It has to do with living a life like Jesus lived and becoming like Him.

Chapter Twenty-Four

COMING TO GOD IN SECRET

"Take heed that you do not do your charitable deeds before men, to be seen by them. Otherwise, you have no reward from your Father in heaven. Therefore, when you do a charitable deed, do not sound a trumpet before you as the hypocrites do in the synagogues and in the streets, that they may have glory from men. Assuredly I say that they have their reward. But when you do a charitable deed, do not let your left hand know what your right hand is doing, that your charitable deed may be in secret; and your Father who sees in secret will reward you openly. And when you pray, you shall not be like the hypocrites. For they love to pray standing in the synagogues and on the corners of the streets, that they may be seen by men. Assuredly, I say to you they have their reward. But you, when you pray, go into your room, and when you have shut the door, pray to your Father who is in the secret place and your Father who sees in secret will reward you openly"
Matthew 6:1-6

Jesus told us in the Sermon on the Mount that we are to come to God in secret. If we give, we are to give in secret, if we fast, we are to fast in secret and if we pray, we are to shut the door and pray in secret and the Father will reward us openly.

A housewife or a mother, or a ditch digger, can hold a higher rank than a world-famous evangelist depending on how their life was lived. Being a mother may seem like a long and tedious role, changing diapers and staying up all night with a sick child, but it is holy ground. Or how about a father who works tirelessly to provide for his family, putting their needs before his own. His years may go by and so do his dreams, but he makes the sacrifice in love. Taking care of the responsibilities God has given you may not get you noticed by the world, but God sees things differently than we do. Remember He rewards the things we do in secret. Something that we may see as little trivial, or lowly, God sees otherwise.

I read such an amazing story in the book, *Visions from Heaven,* by Wendy Alec. In a visitation before the throne of God she describes an amazing story. This particular story comes from a vision she has from heaven. As she is in heaven in the huge assembly before the throne of God, Jesus walks up to someone toward the front. It is a woman. This woman had such an aura of holiness and authority everyone there was awestruck. She seemed like a queen. The angels fell before her and even Jesus bowed to her. Wendy was absolutely held in awe as this woman ascends to the Throne of the Father and actually disappears into His glory.

"Who was she?" she asks Jesus, wondering who would receive such honor, from God before such a huge mass that was gathered.

At this point the woman's life is shown. Her life was tragic. She was born in Scotland during World War One to a single mother and put in an orphanage. She began working at age ten and at age fourteen she was raped by the man of the house. By fifteen she was married to an alcoholic husband who eventually left her to fend for herself with nine children. She worked day and night as a scrub woman to support her children and eventually lost her health and was placed in a workhouse. She was abandoned by all who knew her.

In the workhouse as she was dying someone led her to the Lord and gave her a New Testament. She called on the Lord day and night and was healed. She left the workhouse and again became a maid, but this time no longer alone. She would fellowship with the Father every night in her room. She developed such a relationship of love with Him.

Wendy watched in awe as she watched the woman as she worshiped and prayed, alone in secret, in such love and purity and devotion. Every night in her room they would fellowship and adore each other, she and the Father. She shared with Him her intimate secrets and He with her. Eventually she became blind and died, she was placed in a pauper's grave, and no one was there, she had no one that cared.

Then Wendy is taken to meet her in heaven. She is beautiful, with long black hair to her waist and milky white skin. Her home looks like a palace surrounded by what looked like one hundred acres of gardens filled with roses. Apparently, she had shared with the Father, while on earth her longing for a rose garden,

And the Father was there with her, visiting her as she faithfully visited Him. And Jesus explains to Wendy, "My Father visits her every day at the time of earth's dusk, as she visited Him when she lived on earth."

This woman has a very high position in heaven although

187

on earth she was totally alone and forgotten. She has no visible works, except her years of prayers, which I am sure were effective, but she is unknown even by the church. She has a high place in heaven because she has captivated the heart of the Father with her love and her pure devotion to Him. Even though her life was full of suffering, abuse, hard work and abandonment, she herself became full of love and light. She is one of heaven's queens. Her life was lived in secret. She was unknown by everyone, not one person attended her funeral, but she was cherished by the Father. They had spent many secret hours together. God has chosen to tell her story through Wendy Alec and her life continues to bear fruit even though she is no longer on earth.

This story is so precious to me. It shows what even the loneliest and forgotten person on earth can become. No one is forgotten by God and each of us no matter how incapable we feel, can become what God has called us to become. God rewards those openly who seek Him secretly.

There are many on earth who receive huge accolades and rewards. They dress in clothes that cost more than the average person makes in a year and step on a stage to applause and get a lot of attention. But these rewards will soon be forgotten. How much better is it to be rewarded by God for the things you have given Him? The things no one knew except He and you. Things like your time, your love, or your life poured out for another.

Things done in secret.

Chapter Twenty-Five

A REDEEMED PERSON

We talked earlier about the spirits seen by Neville Johnson and several other visitors to God's throne that hovered around God, asking God, "Can I go to earth? Send me, send me, I want to be a redeemed person!"

These spirits are in a place of incredible beauty and perfection. Why would they beg to come to this dark fallen planet?

Why is it so desirable to be a redeemed person? Why would they {we} want to come to a fallen, cursed planet, with all the pain and suffering and turmoil? Is there something special about being a redeemed person?

Yes, there is. There is nothing quite like us before and there will be nothing like us again. We have an unbelievable opportunity and we wanted to come here. We knowingly have come behind enemy lines and we have knowingly come into Satan's territory. Why?

I believe the future of those who are redeemed from the earth is so great that it is a great honor to be chosen to come to earth. To become a tri-part being and to be created in the image of God and to have the opportunity to follow Christ in a dark world under great opposition. Putting all these factors together the risks are greater, but the rewards are very great.

The rewards are great because the price of our redemption is so very great.

There is something that all the heavenly beings have noticed, something that has their curiosity and interest. The attention of the Father has been caught by those fallen beings on planet earth. All those beings who see Him in all His glory and majesty and have worshipped Him for eons, they see God, His interest is fixed, here on earth. Because of the heart of God being so transfixed on mankind the angels long to serve us.

But there is something even harder for the angels to understand and that is God coming to earth and suffering indescribable things for mankind. Jesus stepped down from His glorious place in heaven to be born into the human race. He changed forms and became human; the very Creator of all things became a lowly human being. The angels watched in awe and wonder. They witnessed His humble birth and saw Him live a humble life.

Satan also finds the Creator of the universe in such a humble position he cannot believe his good fortune. Again, God's love, which Satan sees as His weakness has caused Jesus to come and become vulnerable to him. At first, he is unsuccessful at his attempts to destroy Him, but then finally Satan's day comes. He is finally successful.

He pounces on his opportunity to destroy Jesus. He gathers all the forces of evil and he uses mortal men. He whips them into a fury and uses them to destroy Jesus. They beat Him unmercifully for days. Using whips containing sharp pieces of metal and glass they ripped the flesh from His body. They take canes and beat His head and face causing disfigurement

190

and swelling. They use the fists of men to hit and punch and pull out his beard. They humiliate and mock and spit on Him. They unleash their fury of their sealed fate on the Holy One finally nailing Him to a cross, where His suffering continues until He dies.

Then Satan believes he has won. He takes Jesus to the lowest point of hell where the torture continues. The Father does not act immediately and Satan's confidence soars. He gathers hell together in a great coliseum to make sport of the God they think they have defeated.

The armies of heavens angels are not allowed to make a move. They have been commanded to stand back and watch. They can only watch in horror wondering how this can possibly be happening and why.

This reminds me of a single line I read in the book, *The Final Quest,* by Rick Joyner. Rick is talking to an angel about the crucifixion and the angel says to Rick, *"It is hard for us to understand how our God could suffer like that. It makes us appreciate much more what an honor it is to serve the men for whom He paid such a terrible price."*

The angels are astounded at the price God was willing to pay for us!

As the hordes of hell have gathered to taunt Jesus, on the third day the Father makes His move. The resurrection power of God hit hell like lightning and Jesus the Light of the world lit up every corner of hell and His power destroyed Satan and the principalities and powers of hell. His light burned and destroyed their visages. Then Jesus retrieved the keys of death hell and the grave and resurrected, first to His body and then to heaven where He delivered His atoning blood for us on the mercy seat in heaven. Our redemption was complete!

Satan Fell without Temptation

God had entrusted Satan with much power. Satan was a glorious angel who had access into the very heart of God. Without any temptation Satan fell by his own pride. Satan then was able to convince one third of the angels to follow him in rebellion with him against God. Obviously, God allowed this. He allowed His angels to be tested and He allowed them their own choice. Seeing God in all His splendor as angels do, they were still enticed to follow Satan.

Two Choices

With Satan and his rebellion came a choice. There is no longer just good, there is now good and evil. God operates His kingdom with love. He does not use control or manipulation. God uses love, freedom and He allows choice. God always allows freedom to choose. Love is not love if it is forced. We have the freedom to choose whom we will serve.

Satan allows no freedom. He uses fear, manipulation and control. Satan's subjects hate Satan, and they hate each other. Satan tortures his underlings into submission, and he uses deceit and manipulation to entice his followers. He is a bully and evil beyond words. His cruelty is beyond belief. He actually thinks his ways are more powerful than God's. Those who choose rebellion and to stand with him choose an eternity of torment because that is all Satan has to offer.

God allows freedom to choose because His kingdom operates on love and freedom. The Tree of the Knowledge of

Good and Evil was placed in the Garden of Eden. Adam had the freedom to choose also.

We on this earth, have the freedom to choose God against all odds. What do I mean? On this earth love appears weak. To choose love on this earth is to choose humility. Love turns the other cheek. Love protects the weak and lowly. Love gives to those who are taking. Love returns good for evil. To choose love is to choose God, but it appears weak.

Hate does not have to abide by any rules. It is prideful and unyielding. It steps on anyone who gets in its way and takes instead of gives. It uses the weak for its own gain and thinks nothing of destroying others. It makes huge promises but never pays up. It appears to be strong. Satan is convinced he can overcome love with hate, but he has deceived himself. The Bible tells us love never fails.

Truth also can appear weak and narrow minded. It holds to one path, the only path, there can only be one truth. Like a math problem, two plus two will always equal four, it will never equal five. Truth never changes. But it can appear weak.

The lies are abundant. Deception can be flowery and dressed up and grandiose. They say there are many ways to God. They say freedom of choice. They call sin diversity. Truth can appear so plain next to the dressed up lies of this age. But the deception of this age leads to death.

The way to life is a narrow and difficult path. The road to destruction is easy and wide. To choose God in our life on this earth is to choose to go against the flow, to swim upstream while the world floats effortlessly downstream. To choose to follow Jesus is to choose to crucify your flesh, to pick up your cross and to follow an invisible Savior. A Savior who at times can seem to be a dream, we often wonder if we are crazy.

Sometimes we face ridicule, some have faced death. We are choosing God against all odds. We are laying down our life in a world where it seems like this short life is all we have. We live by faith in a God we cannot see. We follow Him not knowing where we are going. We are fighting an invisible war with invisible enemies and the only way to win is through love and humility.

Whereas Satan fell in the midst of God's glory; we are standing in the midst of hell, never having seen God. We are proving ourselves worthy. We are proving our love for God; we have an opportunity to do the opposite of Satan. Satan fell in the midst of God's glory. We stand in the midst of hell.

And yet all this is building for us something eternal, a character like Christs. Building this character is something eternal that we will never lose. This is a one-time opportunity. It is unique to the suffering that only a fallen planet can provide.

This makes me think of something Rick Joyner wrote in his book called *The Path.* In the book Rick meets two past saints, one is Enoch, and one is Elijah. In this passage Rick is having a conversation with Elijah. Rick notices a difference between Elijah and Enoch, and he asks Elijah about it. I will quote the book.

"You walked with God too, and you were trusted with some of the greatest power He ever revealed through a prophet. Why aren't you as joyful as Enoch?" I inquired.

I don't mind your asking, and this is important for you to understand. What you become in your life on earth will be who you are forever, without the carnality of course. If anyone on earth realized how much their life on earth

impacted their eternity, they would be in pursuit of the fruit of the Spirit more than any earthly treasure or accomplishment.

"The greatest treasure in all of creation is love. Love is the foundation of true joy and peace and is the essence of what man was created to be. God is love, and if you walk with Him as you are called to, this will be your portion."

Elijah then explains that walking during the dark difficult times on earth caused him to let the evil overshadow the love he should have had. He talked about calling the fire down on people and delighting in it instead of weeping for them as he should have been doing. Elijah explains that Enoch, who also lived in a time of horrific evil kept his focus on loving God and walking with him. Enoch was a man of joy and hope. These qualities became eternal. Then later Elijah says something profound to Rick.

"Those who are known as the great ones on earth are not always well-known in heaven. Those who are known as great ones in heaven are those who love the most."

So back to our point, to be a redeemed person is a high honor. We have chosen God against all odds. We have the choice to be as close to God as we want to be and go as far in God as we are willing to pay the price. Enoch was a champion of this. Because of the way Enoch lived he never died.

You were chosen to come to earth. You have been given the opportunity to become a redeemed person. God highly values His redeemed. Jesus said that He would leave the ninety-nine sheep to find the one lost sheep. We on earth are the lost sheep. Jesus said that he who has been forgiven much, loves much.

Redeemed mankind is the greatest mystery.

Yes, we were dead in sin, but we have been made alive in Christ!

Yes, we are weak, but our weakness has been replaced with His strength!

Yes, we were without hope but now we have an eternal hope. We have an inheritance; and we have been adopted into the family of God. We are a new creation. We are a royal priesthood. We have the Holy Spirit of God dwelling within us. This was God's plan and we have become a part of it, we have become a redeemed person!

Chapter Twenty-Six

LEARNING TO THINK DIFFERENTLY

Remember in the introduction of this book, when I first became a Christian and I thought I had God in my pocket, and I was almost smug? And then as time went on, I realized I knew very little about God. I had to learn to think differently about God. I had to realize that there was so much I did not know. God was so much different than what I had first thought. I recently heard a vision told online by Terry Bennet. He said he was taken to a place in outer space, and he saw sand, a huge amount of sand. He said there was all the sand in the universe represented here, a vast amount of sand. The Lord was holding one grain of sand in His hand, and He told Terry, "This one grain of sand represents all that is known. The rest of the sand you see represents all that is yet to be known."

I gasped when I heard this. There is just so much we don't know about God about ourselves and about everything!

This absolutely blew my mind!

Then Terry said, "It is not about what you know but Who you know."

I gasped again as I let this sink in. I can't possibly begin to know what God knows; He knows all. But I can trust Him and trust Him to show me what I do need to know.

I have been pressing into God for more than forty years now and the same thing just keeps on happening. I start to think I know something about God and my mind gets blown again. And not only that, I realize that being created in His image is also mind blowing, I find out that we are amazing creatures because we have been made in His image, there is more to us than we realize, and more to come. This is beyond comprehension.

It happened again about a week ago.

I love going to sleep at night. I feel God's presence when it gets dark and quiet. And sometimes He wakes me up and His presence is even thicker. Well, that happened the other night. I woke up and He was so there. I felt a vibration and a power coursing through me. And I felt His huge presence.

I thought about what Neville Johnson said in one of his sermons, I wrote about it in chapter 11. He said that he was taken out to the very edge of the universe, and he saw the universe from afar and it was in the shape of a man. And I thought about how each of the billions of solar systems resemble an atom, with the particles spinning around the nucleus, like planets spinning around their suns. And I remembered hearing from quantum physics how in atoms, there is just as much empty space between particles as the outer space between stars, we only feel solid, but we have a lot of empty space.

I started wondering if the universe was Him.

As I was laying there thinking like this the Lord said to me, "Each person is a tiny replica of Me."

As He said this, I felt energy and power coursing through me. I felt in awe and wondered how much I didn't know about myself. I tend to only think about now, but we have a marvelous future unfolding with God that is incredible beyond belief.

I heard Neville say it in a sermon the other day. He said cats produce cats and dogs produce dogs, but God produces gods. We are created to be like Him.

No wonder Satan hates us so. He knew he could never be what we were created to be. He is only an angel and that is all he would ever be. He doesn't have the creative power within that has been placed in us. He needs to use fallen man to create with; he cannot do this on his own.

We have a future beyond imagination. We are God's kids. We cannot comprehend what that means. Jesus talked about the faithful ruling cities. There are eons to come and a huge universe out there. What are we going to be doing?

There is so much to learn not only about God but about ourselves. We only function now at a tiny capacity of what we will function at. We are like infants who have no idea what is to come, we just cling to our parents, and they know what we can't yet.

My daughter, Joy had a conversation with God the other night. The Father told her, "You are present here in heaven through My Son. And He is present on earth through you. You need to be more present in heaven and He needs to be more present on earth.   "

Wow! I love this stuff!

We are not yet walking in what we are capable of, we have no idea what we are capable of. We can be present in heaven and earth simultaneously. What else? It all seems beyond belief; things are so much different than we could possibly imagine. And speaking of imagination, our imaginations are real. Just like God we have a world on the inside and a world on the outside.

It all comes back to Jesus, our Creator and our Redeemer. Pursuing Him is the bottom line. We are running a race on this earth; the same one He ran. We are to be looking unto Him the Author and Finisher of Our faith. He is love and we must become love. He was the light of the world and now we are. He was transfigured on top of a mountain in the presence of Peter James and John, and we must also change.

I find that I have to constantly expand my thinking about God, about me, about everything. I amaze myself at how ridiculous I have been {and still am} when I think I get to this level that I really know how things are. I have done it with the Bible also. I have read it through many times, and I thought I knew what was in there. I have since learned I haven't a clue. I heard someone say in a sermon the Bible has seven levels of truth. Some levels we will not even get to in this age, but they are for ages to come.

What that means is what we are reading has layers of truth and meanings; there is much more than just what you read on the surface.   There is just so much in there!!!!

I have to be ready to think differently because there is so much, I don't know. Actually, there is too much to know. So, I need to know Him, more and more and more, because He knows everything!

Chapter Twenty-Seven

COMING HOME

So, we found out a magnificent secret.

We are so fearfully and wonderfully made. God is so much more than our minds can comprehend and yet He has made us in His image. We came from Him. We lived in Him. Before we had a body or a soul our spirit lived inside of His heart, and He knew us. His heart was our home. Then He created the physical plane for us, the universe and the earth. He put us here and made us a tri-part being, like Himself. We had the capability to exist in the physical world and the spiritual world. We had the ability to rule the earth and fellowship with God and actually walk with him in the cool of the day. But when our forefather, Adam fell, we all fell. We had no hope until Jesus came and became the second Adam. He redeemed us. Now we are a new creation, a redeemed person.

Our magnificent secret is the Holy Spirit is living on the inside of us. This wonder of wonders and our potential is incredible. The Holy Spirit searches all things, He knows everything. Like a magnificent search engine, He knows everything about everything, He is all knowing. And He knows all about us. He knows what is stored in our conscious mind and even our subconscious mind. He is with you and in you and He knows how to fix you. He is our Teacher, our Comforter, and He even helps us pray. God is in us!

We are a wonder, even to the angels. Even the angels consider it an honor to be chosen to serve us, because of our position with God! They desire to look into our salvation. We are an amazement to all the beings that came before us. They stand back and wonder, what is man?

God has made us in His image, the image of the Father, the Son and the Holy Spirit. He has placed inside of us parts of Himself, His talents, His imagination and ability to create and even His emotions. But it is more than that because our being is much like His being, our spirit man, resembles the Father and carries His light and from our being flows His living water. And our soul is a layered being which is extremely complex and is able to be in heaven and on earth at the same time. Our soul is created like the Holy Spirit. And our body will soon be resurrected and have supernatural power like Jesus' body does.   And we are His body on earth.

We have found that we exist in God. That means we are present in Him in the past, the present and the future. When He looks at us, He sees all three. Yes, right now we are walking through the sands of time, but the day will come when we will also be outside of time.

We have learned that God is a God of incredible detail. He has detailed plans called DNA on the inside of your body with all the information on how your body is to look, develop and function. The details are amazing and precise and written out the information would reach around the sun and back. But that is just your body. He has planned your life and everything about it. He planned when you would be born, where and to whom. He has detailed plans for every day you spend on earth. But it goes farther than that it reaches forward to eons to come.

But yet there is more! God's attention is fixed on this earth, this fallen planet, where incredible evil exists. Yes, there is danger here, but He is here with you. He has a plan for this planet and we who live on it. The future for earth is incredible, soon there will be a thousand-year reign with Jesus as king reigning from Jerusalem, the capitol of the earth. And then from there the New Jerusalem comes down from heaven, and earth becomes the capital of the universe, and God dwells with us. And who reigns with Him but those who were faithful in this special time. We were chosen for this.

But what about the pain and the suffering we experience on earth? Doesn't He know? Does he care?

Yes, God has allowed pain and suffering for a time, but He is right here with us, hidden by a veil. There is nothing that you will experience that He will not experience with you.

When you experience pain, it is nothing like the pain He is experiencing. His is much worse. You have never been alone. It is not just the angels assigned to you caring for you, His presence hovers over you continually, He is feeling everything you feel. Not a tear falls from your eyes that He has not saved in a bottle.

God's attention is completely here on this planet because His children are here. He has allowed us the honor and the privilege to know Him and to choose our destiny.

To choose to believe in a God we do not see. His presence is veiled at this time, we see Him dimly with the eyes of faith.

To choose His love which only in this realm appears weak. His love, the greatest power in the universe, comes wrapped in humility. When it is reviled it does not revile in return.

To choose to follow His light which in this realm can be overshadowed by the dark neon lights of the world that appears to offer pleasure, but in the end is only brokenness. In His eternal light is love, joy and peace.

To choose His truth among the multiple lies that try to drown it out. His truth never changes, it stands the eternal test of time unlike the popular thinking of the world which continually changes with the times. His truth stands plain against the overdressed lies of the enemy.

And to choose the narrow path that Jesus walked when He walked this earth which led to suffering and a cross.

We have this choice.

Yes, we live in a fallen world. Many around us deny that God exists. Many rail at Him in anger and actually defy Him.

Many choose to follow Satan in their hatred of God and in doing so they embrace evil. Human minds inspired by Satan have become so vile it is beyond belief. Things our grandparents shunned are now being paraded in the streets. Babies are ripped from their mother's wombs. Children are sold into slavery to be used as sex objects.

All of us have taken part in the evil in this world some more than others. We have done evil to others, but we have also had evil done to us. We have been hurt and betrayed, abused and have suffered much pain. We know about sickness and fear and about strife. There are accidents here and disasters of every kind, man-made and natural and it evens gets worse, there is murder and war and terrorism. This world is a dark place, and it keeps getting darker. There are those who wish that they had never been born!

Because of this some actually judge God! They decide that evil comes from Him and that He is unjust! For this reason, they reject Him. They have put themselves on the side of evil and have aligned with Satan. We cannot judge God! We also cannot accuse God of evil. He is incapable of evil. We also have to quit waiting for God to come and do our job for us. It is the body of Christ's job on earth to overcome evil with good. Remember the Sermon on the Mount; we are actually supposed to be doing this stuff.

And there is something else, whether we remember it or not. We asked to come here. We came here with a purpose just as Jesus did. One time when I first became a Christian and I was struggling the Lord Jesus spoke to me audibly. I had suddenly become despondent in my thoughts and was speaking to the Lord in my thoughts and telling Him I would never make it. To my surprise He answered me audibly and said, "I will take you every step of the way."

I was surprised but what struck me the most was that His voice was so familiar. I felt like I knew it from before. It was stirring in my memory that I had heard that voice long ago, at the beginning of my existence. I have cherished those words but ever since that day I have longed to hear His audible voice again. It gave me such a wonderful feeling.

We once existed as a spirit inside of God and we asked to come here to be a redeemed person. And we were chosen. And we were chosen for this particular time also, the time most desired by all, when the greatest battles are just ahead. We wanted a chance for the High Calling in Christ!

I heard of a vision that Bob Jones had before he died. If

you haven't heard of Bob Jones, he was one of the greatest prophets of our time. He was closely involved with Morningstar Ministries.

Bob Jones saw a vision of the great spiritual leaders of the past, people like Mariah Woodworth Etter and Smith Wigglesworth and many others, he saw them on a beach. Each one would come and bend down and start digging in the sand. They were searching for something, but they did not find it. They looked disappointed and walked away.

Then he would see another of the great leaders from the past come and do the same, each of them dug but found nothing and walked away dejected. Then God told Bob to go down. Bob went down and he put his hands in the sand, and he felt something. He dug it up and it was a great treasure chest. Bob opened it.

The treasure chest was filled with millions of pieces of paper with names on them. God told Bob that these were the names of those chosen to be in the end time army. This is what the great leaders of the past desired, this is what they were looking for. The longings of the generations ahead of us was to be where we are in this end time army, but it was given for us at this time.

Our greatest battles are just ahead of us. We have been chosen to live in this day and this hour. This is the greatest time to be chosen to live. Those who walked before us have desired to see this day.

If we look with our natural eyes, we will not see this. We will see the world in upheaval. We will see Satan trying to win his doomed war against God. We will see incredible evil and darkness.

We have to look with our spiritual eyes. We have to

remember who we are and that we asked to be here, we wanted this chance! We have to remember Who our Father is, and that we were created in His image, and more than that we are a redeemed person and the Trinity dwells inside of us through the person of the Holy Spirit.

God has placed us here to rule and reign with Him, and to win a war the way He wins wars, the way Jesus won the greatest battle and the way Jesus taught us to, with His words and His example, the way that is written in the words in red in the four gospels and especially the Sermon on the Mount, with love, with truth, with humility and with laying our lives down in obedience.

I have several hopes for you my reader, hopes that as you read this book you will see things differently.

I hope I have made God bigger to you. I hope you are beginning to see He is much more than we can possibly realize. He is bigger and more powerful and more complex. Everything you see is His handiwork, the earth, the sky, the oceans and all the creatures, the heavens and the billions of galaxies. Look around you and see everything He has made and then realize everything you see exists in Him.

Now look again and make Him bigger. He also exists simultaneously in the past, in the present and in the future. There is nowhere that He doesn't exist. The reality of God, His power and His glory is everywhere. His presence is very real, everything pales in comparison. He is in you and around you and you are standing in Him, and He is big.

I hope I have made God bigger. I hope you are feeling new and different. When you breathe in and when you breathe out, I hope you realize He is the life and breath within you. I hope He also is becoming bigger inside of you as you are becoming more aware of Him.

I hope also that you are realizing who you are. You came from Him, and you will return to Him. To return to God is to come home, where you once existed, in His heart. You are a chip off a giant block. You are in His image.

I hope you are being filled with a feeling of awe and wonder, about God, about yourself, about the world you live in and about your future in the eons to come. I hope you feel a difference in the very atmosphere around you.

Remember my dream, the dream I told you about in chapter 11. I drove through a tunnel into a huge mountain. The mountain was so strong and the thick rock walls and once inside I felt such awe and wonder. I wanted to go there again, and I wanted to take you there.

In the mountain was a different atmosphere. It felt wonderful. It was a mixture of peace, a lot of peace, joy, wonder, awe and excitement. My heart beat faster and I felt breathless. The feeling was calm and excitement at once. It was delicious. In fact, I feel it now and I have felt as I have worked on this book. It's a feeling of being in God.

My hope is that I have pulled back the veil and that I have brought you into this mountain. I hope that you have come home. You exist in God and God exists in you. I hope that I have opened your eyes to the wonder of who God is and to the wonder of who you are, you are fearfully and wonderfully made. You were created to rule and to reign with Him.

There is no other creation like a redeemed person. We are unique. We have great potential. And most of all we belong, we belong to God. We came from Him; we look like Him and we exist in Him. When we return to Him, we return to where we came from, we come Home.

Epilogue

Dear Readers,

I want to always give you the opportunity to come to the Lord if you don't yet know Him. Would you like the unbelievable honor and privilege to become a redeemed person? It means to come face to face with Jesus and follow Him instead of the way of this world. Jesus went before you and died on the cross for you so that you can be redeemed. Now your part is to come to Him and choose. Pray with me,

Jesus, please forgive me for my sins. I choose You. Please redeem by Your blood. I give You, my life. Thank you for creating me in Your image, please help me to become more and more like You. Amen,

You have started on a journey that leads you down a narrow path, but the path you are on leads to a glorious future that never ends.

Notes

Chapter 4 *The Heavens Opened* by Anna Rountree

Creation House, Lake Mary, Florida 32746

Page 88

My Time in Heaven, by Richard Sigmund

Whitaker House, New Kensington, PA 15068

Page 109

Heaven, Close Encounters of the God Kind
by Jesse Duplantis   Harrison House,
Tulsa, Oklahoma

Page 114

Chapter 9 *The Heavens Opened* by Anna Rountree

Creation House, Lake Mary, Florida 32746

Page 103

Heaven, Close Encounters of the God Kind,
by Jesse Duplantis

Harrison House, Tulsa Oklahoma

Page 119

Chapter 10 The *Heavens Opened* by Anna Rountree

Creation House, Lake Mary, Florida

Pages 36-37

Chapter 25 The *Path,* by Rick Joyner, copyright 2013

Used by permission, www.morningstarministries.org

Page 186